Wealth with Faith

Overcome Money Blocks and Achieve
Financial Freedom using Islamic Strategies

SARAH GULFRAZ

Copyright © 2024 Sarah Gulfraz

Sarah Gulfraz has asserted her right to be identified as the author of this Work in accordance with the Copyright, Designs and Patents Act 1988.

All rights reserved.

No portion of this book may be reproduced in any form, stored in a retrieval system, stored in a database, or published/transmitted in any form or by any means, electronic, mechanical, photocopying, recording or otherwise, without prior written permission of the publisher.

Dedication

~ Bismillah ~

May Allah (swt) accept our efforts and grant us success in this life and the next. Ameen.

In dedication to my loving family and all their support.

Contents

1. Introduction — 1
2. Introduction to Money Mindset and Islamic Principles — 3
3. Recognising Money Blocks and Limiting Beliefs — 17
4. Overcoming Fear and Scarcity Mindset — 28
5. Developing a Proactive Money Mindset — 38
6. Islamic Perspective on Earning Halal Income — 52
7. Budgeting and Financial Planning in Islam — 66
8. Overcoming Debt and Managing Financial Obligations — 80
9. Investing Wisely According to Sharia Principles — 92
10. Generosity and Charity in Wealth Management — 100
11. Building Long-Term Financial Stability — 109
12. Conclusion — 116

Find Out More — 118

Chapter One

Introduction

The financial landscape is changing dramatically all around us, certainly much more quickly than we fully realise and far faster than it has in the past.

Numerous causes are driving change, including the power of ever-growing technical improvement and economic advances. Wealth management and financial stability are two major concerns that most people are talking about nowadays.

This world is undoubtedly fast-paced, consumer-driven, and always changing. It is simple to become distracted by the pursuit of money and other belongings and forget the real purpose of our lives as Muslims. Fortunately, the principles of Islam offer us a guide to assist us in striking a balance between our financial security and our religious beliefs.

As Muslims, we are urged to consider our wealth in light of Islamic teachings, which strongly emphasise utilising one's possessions for the good of others and the pursuit of spiritual development.

> *Allah (SWT) says in the Quran: "And whoever obeys Allah (SWT) and His Messenger and fears Allah (SWT) and is conscious of Him – it is those who are the successful ones." (Quran 24:52)*

The aforementioned verse clarifies that meeting one's spiritual needs is essential to success and should not be disregarded. Therefore, Muslims must follow a strategy for success based on Islamic teachings. For Muslims, the path to financial success is directly connected with clear guidelines that ensure wealth is earned, spent, and invested in ways that strictly align with Islamic values.

Yet, nobody can say that they've never encountered difficulties. Many of us struggle with money blocks, limiting beliefs, and the fear of scarcity, often feeling trapped in financial stress. Our ability to effectively confront and resolve these issues can affect our daily lives; hence, maintaining a balance between wealth and faith is required.

This book aims to help its readers gain guidance on managing their finances and achieving financial independence through faith-based strategies. Through this comprehensive guidance, they can handle the financial barriers by applying Islamic principles to their financial journey.

For Muslims, the Quran and Hadith are considered the best sources that provide ethical guidelines through which they can not only overcome financial obstacles but also grow their wealth in a halal (permissible) way.

Through each chapter of this book, you'll gain practical insights for managing your money in ways that honour Islamic ethics. This book will provide the tools to achieve financial stability while staying grounded in your faith.

Chapter Two

Introduction to Money Mindset and Islamic Principles

Understanding Money Mindset in the Context of Islamic Ethics

While owning a large house and expensive cars is good, and there is nothing inherently wrong with appreciating beautiful things, one's ultimate objective should not be material abundance alone.

One of the countless benefits Allah (SWT) has given humanity is wealth, and there are various ways to acquire it. However, Islam offers proper guidelines for attaining wealth, encouraging Muslims to pursue it through lawful (halal) means.

Undoubtedly, earning money is a significant factor in giving life purpose in human existence. Islam firmly directs Muslims to ensure that the source of earning money must be pure, ethical, and free from any prohibited (haram) activities.

However, as Muslims, we strive to live our lives by Islamic values, including our spending and earning. So, our earnings and expenditures must remain within the boundaries of Islam.

As Muslims, we are all aware that our purpose for existing is to worship Allah (SWT). The Muslim goal in life shouldn't be restricted to working till one dies to gain greater wealth and position. This life is fleeting, after all.

Nonetheless, it is still true that to support oneself and one's family, one must seek a halal income. Since Allah (SWT) is Ar-Razzaq (the Provider), we should look for halal sources of income. At the same time, we must remember to work hard for it; food won't just appear on our tables, and the bills won't pay themselves.

Understanding the "money mindset" according to Islamic teachings offers clear guidance on earning from halal ways for wealth acquisition, distribution, and ethical conduct related to finances. A "money mindset" refers to how Muslims manage their money in ways compliant with Islamic principles.

Definition of money mindset and its impact on financial decisions

Before understanding what a money mindset is, it's necessary to know as a Muslim what money in Islam is. The use of money as a medium of exchange is widely acknowledged. This means that money serves as a fundamental unit of account, enabling money to assign prices and values to objects, facilitating trade and the exchange of goods and services.

At the same time, according to Islamic law, money can only be used as a means of exchange—that is, to pay for the goods and services we need and want. What form of money is allowed in Islam? Firstly, gold and silver are referenced explicitly in the Quran.

> *Allah (SWT) says in the Quran: "The enjoyment of worldly desires—women, children, treasures of gold and silver, fine horses, cattle, and fertile land—has been made appealing to people. These are the pleasures of this worldly life, but with Allah (SWT) is the finest destination." (Quran 3:14)*

This does not imply, however, that gold and silver are the exclusive forms of money. Renowned philosopher Ibn Taymiyyah suggests that Sharia does not precisely explain what money is; rather, this has been left up to the traditional practices of the people.

The main concern for Muslims is not what money is. Instead, the important question that weighs the Islamic perspective is, "Is money evil or good?" Discussions on money can be touchy and spark polarisation. Many people consider pursuing financial success "selfish" and "greedy."

However, we must first clarify the Islamic perspective on wealth to fully comprehend the "money mindset". Islam does not sit at any end of this scale. Rather, we think Allah (SWT) is the rightful owner of all riches. Wealth is bestowed upon Muslims as a trial as well as a blessing. Regardless of our financial situation, Allah (SWT) will interrogate us about how we made and used our money on the Day of Judgment (Akirah).

In Islam, having a lot of money could be considered a benefit, provided it is used for Allah's (SWT) will and to support one's obedience to Him. However, it could be disastrous if applied evilly, causing someone to become haughty and conceited or diverting their attention from remembering and obeying Allah (SWT).

The money mindset, as per Islam, revolves around an understanding of money or wealth that aligns with the teachings of the Quran and Sunnah, which emphasise ethical conduct, social justice, and spiritual well-being.

> *Allah (SWT) says in the Quran: "Made beautiful for mankind is the love of desires for women and offspring, of hoarded heaps of gold and silver, of branded horses, cattle and plantations." (Quran 3:14)*

> *"O Children of Adam! Dress properly whenever you are at worship. Eat and drink, but do not waste. Surely He does not like the wasteful. Ask, O Prophet (PBUH), "Who has forbidden the adornments and lawful provisions Allah (SWT) has brought forth for His servants?" Say, "They are for the enjoyment of the believers in this worldly life, but they will be exclusively theirs on the Day of Judgment. This is how we make Our revelations clear for people of knowledge." (Quran 7:31-32)*

The above verses highlight the balance between enjoying the provisions of this world and avoiding excess or waste, encouraging Muslims to maintain a spiritual and ethical approach to wealth in line with Islamic values.

In Islam, praying for sufficient halal rizq, good provision, and nourishment is not only permissible but it is encouraged. In fact, striving for a lawful livelihood is considered a virtue. It is also improper for male family members who provide for the family not to work.

Allah (SWT) requires humanity to struggle for anything they need. Our rizq is here in the world for us to find, thanks to Allah (SWT). To find it, we need to work for it in the same way that food on your kitchen table isn't going to come to you while you're lying on the sofa.

Hence, efforts are mandatory to earn halal money. That implies that whichever route you choose, put your best effort into your work. Assume the role of the most competent person that you can be. Choose the route that will get you closer to Allah (SWT) and help you become an expert in your field if you want to earn halal money.

> *Prophet (PBUH) said: "By him in whose hand is my soul if one of you were to carry a bundle of firewood on his back and sell it, that would be better for him than begging a man who may or may not give him anything." (Sahih Bukhari)*

In Islam, a money mindset involves viewing wealth as a trust from Allah (SWT) and managing it ethically. It emphasises earning through permissible means, avoiding interest and unethical practices, and balancing material needs with spiritual goals.

Muslims are encouraged to invest in alignment with Islamic principles, prioritise charity, manage debt responsibly, and save prudently. This mindset fosters gratitude and contentment, ensuring financial decisions support personal well-being and communal welfare while adhering to moral guidelines. Overall, it integrates financial management with faith, promoting a responsible and balanced approach to wealth.

Importance of aligning financial beliefs with Islamic teachings

Islamic teachings give us a guide to assist us in striking a balance between our financial security and our faith. Let's examine the values and viewpoints that stem from Islamic teachings and support a sensible approach to financial security.

When it comes to wealth, we, as Muslims, are encouraged to take a balanced approach. Although it is easy to become obsessed with the need to support oneself, in the end, Allah (SWT) is the one who provides. Financial contentment comes from earning for the hereafter, not this life. Financial uneasiness arises from focusing on earning money for this life.

It is in our nature as humans to have an extraordinary affection for wealth. The Quran tells us this, and the Prophet (PBUH) cautions against the responsibilities of being extremely wealthy and abusing it.

We Muslims believe in rizq, Allah's (SWT) provision of nourishment. In addition to being a way for us to support our families and ourselves, this rizq is an assessment from Allah (SWT), who has the power to either strengthen our bonds with Him or drive us away.

Islamic teachings, which strongly emphasise using one's resources for the good of others and the pursuit of spiritual development, encourage Muslims to view wealth through this perspective. Based on the idea of rizq, this viewpoint encourages Muslims to acknowledge that all wealth ultimately belongs to Allah (SWT) and to be humble and grateful for what they have.

Our income and expenditures must remain within the guidelines of Islam as Muslims. We are instructed to practise ethical and responsible consumerism and to avoid haram sources of revenue, including interest, gambling, and illegal trading.

Islam prohibits being frugal or overspending on oneself when it comes to money. We must practise moderation in our spending and allocate a percentage of our fortune to charity and family. This might be considered a form of charity if done with the correct motivation.

By applying these concepts to our financial lives, we may use these resources to better ourselves, our families, and society at large. We will also be more successful in the hereafter and feel more content and fulfilled. Regardless of one's religious background, these guidelines are also helpful for anyone looking for a more ethical and holistic approach to personal economics.

Overview of Islamic Principles on Wealth and Money Management

As Muslims, we work hard every day to cultivate the spiritual qualities necessary for this life and the next. However, we also require financial resources to purchase the material goods we need in this life. How does Islam advise us on obtaining and using wealth?

We know Allah (SWT) is the source of anything we need, including wealth, and everything else in the universe is his property. How, then, do we allocate our riches appropriately? Let's look at Islamic principles on wealth and money management.

These principles derived from the Quran and the Hadith (sayings and practices of the Prophet Muhammad (PBUH)) are designed to ensure fairness, justice, and social welfare. Here are some key principles:

Wealth as trust (Amanah)

According to the Quran, wealth is a form of trust from Allah (SWT), in line with the role and purpose of human beings. Since humans have been designated as Allah's (SWT) servants and vicegerents on Earth (khalifahs), money ultimately belongs to Allah (SWT) alone and is bestowed upon them based on trust.

Therefore, as part of their roles as khalifahs, humans have the right to accumulate, manage, and use wealth, which comes with complete accountability.

As humans, we are predisposed to love wealth and accumulate it because that is how we have been created. Thus, there is a close relationship between the accumulation of riches and human character. The Quran characterises this inclination as a test, warning individuals not to get too caught up in material possessions since they are merely an embellishment or a source of consolation for this life.

Enjoy wealth, but try not to let it divert you.

Although wealth might make us happy, it can also divert our attention from the things that matter. Since riches cannot accompany a believer into the afterlife, a sincere believer treats it as if it were only material. The Quran forbids greed, cautioning Muslims against it. Rather than accumulating large sums of money, Muslims should give it away to those in need.

Moral consumption is preferred.

Ensuring that our earnings and expenditures align with Islamic guidelines is crucial. As well as being instructed to practise moral and prudent consumption, we are also warned against haram sources of money. Overspending on oneself or being frugal is not acceptable in Islam. We must spend wisely, allocate some of our riches to charitable causes, and spend a reasonable amount on our families. This could be considered charitable giving if done with the proper intent.

It is never appropriate to live off of wrongdoing.

Muslims must work for their riches in a halal (or legal) manner. This means not obtaining wealth by selling or purchasing items that Allah (SWT) forbids us from having, like pork or alcohol, or by taking part in unlawful activity. Allah (SWT) says:

> "O you who have believed, do not consume one another's wealth unjustly but only [in lawful] business by mutual consent." (Quran 4:29)

Prohibition of Interest (Riba)

Islam strictly prohibits the charging and paying of interest (Riba). Interest is seen as exploitative, creating inequality and harming the less privileged. Islamic financial systems are structured around profit-sharing, leasing, and partnership models (like Mudarabah and Musharakah), where both risk and reward are shared.

Wealth redistribution through Charity

Giving is essential to an Islamic economy in full bloom. Zakat, a required charitable donation, is one of our five pillars. This system's beauty is that philanthropy benefits both the giver and the recipient. Giving money away with the proper aim fosters gratitude, empathy, and compassion.

> *The Prophet Muhammad (PBUH) said: "Whoever pays the zakat on his wealth will have its evil removed from him." (Ibn Majah)*

This hadith shows how Zakat purifies wealth, benefiting both the giver by removing spiritual harm and the recipient by fulfilling their needs. Muslims are urged to donate to charity freely (Sadaqah) in addition to Zakat, with the notion that generosity grows and purifies one's wealth rather than reduces it. Giving away money we have earned can serve as a shield against materialism and conceit, two detrimental effects of prosperity.

Notion of Barakah

Barakah, or divine benefits, is central to Islamic wealth and money management. With the help of Barakah, our wealth can be more valuable, productive, and efficient. Muslims may bring Barakah into their lives and achieve greater happiness, fulfilment, and success in their financial endeavours by looking for halal income and spending opportunities.

Barakah describes riches in terms of its influence, quality, and amount. Being content with one's belongings, fulfilling one's requirements on a modest income, or witnessing one's wealth positively impact others are just a few examples of how Barakah manifests itself. Adhering to Islamic rules in all facets of financial life—from income to expenditure and all points in between—is the secret to drawing Barakah.

Emphasis on transparency and honesty

Islam values honesty, transparency, and fairness in all financial dealings. Deception, fraud, and unfair practices in business or financial transactions are prohibited, and clear contracts are encouraged to prevent disputes.

These principles encourage financial and economic practices that promote fairness, social justice, and the community's well-being, reflecting Islam's broader ethical and moral framework.

Quranic verses and Prophetic traditions (Hadith) related to wealth and finance

The Quran and the Hadith (Prophetic traditions) provide numerous teachings on wealth, finance, and ethical and economic behaviour. Below are some key Quranic verses and Hadiths related to wealth and finance.

Wealth is considered a blessing from Allah (SWT), but it is also seen as a test of how one uses it—whether to help others or for selfish purposes.

> *"Righteousness is not that you turn your faces toward the east or the west, but [true] righteousness is in one who believes in Allah (SWT), the Last Day, the Angels, the Book, and the Prophets and gives his wealth, in spite of love for it, to relatives, orphans, the needy, the traveller, those who ask [for help], and for freeing slaves; [and who] establishes prayer and gives zakah..." (Quran 2:177)*

> *"Believe in Allah (SWT) and His Messenger and spend out of that in which He has made you successors. For those who have believed among you and spent, there will be a great reward." (Quran 57:7)*

Zakat is one of the Five Pillars of Islam. It is a compulsory charity meant to purify wealth and help those in need.

> *"The Prophet (PBUH) said: 'The best charity is that which is given when one is in need and struggling." (Sahih Bukhari)*

Moreover, Islam promotes honesty and fairness in business dealings and condemns fraud, deception, and dishonest gain.

> *"Woe to those who give less [than due], who when they take a measure from people, take in full. But if they give by measure or by weight to them, they cause loss." (Quran 83:1-3)*

Islam encourages a balanced lifestyle, neither extreme poverty nor extravagance, but rather moderation in spending. "

> *"And they who, when they spend, do so not excessively or sparingly but are ever, between that, [justly] moderate." (Quran 25:67)*

In addition to Zakat, Islam encourages voluntary charity (Sadaqah) to help the poor and needy, which brings blessings in both this world and the Hereafter.

> The Prophet (PBUH) said: "The upper hand is better than the lower hand. The upper hand is the one that gives, and the lower hand is the one that takes." (Sahih Bukhari)

These teachings form the ethical foundation for wealth management and financial transactions in Islamic tradition, promoting a system of fairness and responsibility.

Ethics of Earnings in Islam

Our relationship with Allah (SWT) is one of the most important parts of our lives, and it is impacted by the way we earn, spend, and manage our income. Allah (SWT) cleanses our riches and shields us from the negative effects of engaging in haram (forbidden) or illegal activities when we maintain our wealth halal.

Allah (SWT) also increases the influence of halal wealth, making it more productive and advantageous for ourselves and those around us. Thus, our financial duty as Muslims is to manage our wealth in a halal manner and invest it for the well of our community, ourselves, and the generations that will follow us in this life and the next. So, how do we ensure that our money is halal?

Halal vs Haram Money

Earned income, in accordance with Islamic teachings, is referred to as halal money. It does not include profits from illicit operations like the manufacturing of alcohol, gambling, or usury. Obtaining halal money also entails moral behaviour, such as dealing fairly and preventing harm to others, which synchronises financial operations with social and moral obligations.

The two main sources of Islamic teachings, the Quran and the Hadith, strongly emphasise making money legally and abstaining from immoral behaviour. This is not only for one's spiritual development but also for the welfare of the community at large.

Halal money refers to wealth obtained in accordance with Islamic law and morality. The idea of earning a living via sincere and diligent labour while abstaining from actions deemed haram or prohibited is strongly associated with this concept. This covers activities including interest-based trades, gambling, and lying or fraud.

Halal money can be made in various ways. Among the most popular ones are launching one's own company, working in the halal sector, purchasing halal goods for agriculture, and purchasing halal real estate. Real estate investment trusts (REITs), mutual funds, and halal stock are just a few options for halal savings and investing.

Individuals should carefully examine which of these possibilities best fits their requirements and aspirations, as each has a unique mix of opportunities and problems.

> *"O you who have believed, do not consume one another's wealth unjustly or send it [in bribery] to the rulers in order that [they might aid] you [to] consume a portion of the wealth of the people in sin, while you know [it is unlawful]." (Quran 2:188)*

This verse emphasises that wealth should be earned lawfully, without injustice or deception, and forbids gaining wealth through unlawful means.

On the other hand, haram earnings refer to income generated through means forbidden by Islamic law (Sharia). These earnings violate ethical principles and are considered impure and unlawful. Below are some of the common forms of haram earnings:

Riba (Usury): Riba refers to unjust and exploitative gains, such as excessive interest on loans or unequal exchanges. It opposes Islamic teachings, where wealth should be earned through fair effort and shared risk. As Allah (SWT) says: *"Allah has permitted trade and forbidden interest." (Quran 2:275)*

Bribery: Prophet Muhammad (PBUH) said: *"The worst unlawful earning is the income a governor gains through bribery."* Bribery disrupts justice, erodes trust, and leads to corruption. *(Ibn Majah)*

Profiteering: Cheating and overpricing are forbidden. Allah (SWT) warns: *"Woe to those who give less [than due]." (Quran 83:1-3)*

Ultimately, Muslims who strive to earn a halal source of income pave the way for personal fulfilment, spiritual growth, and communal well-being. This approach ensures that wealth is gained in a manner that is both righteous and beneficial for all.

Chapter Three

Recognising Money Blocks and Limiting Beliefs

Identifying Common Money Blocks in the Muslim Community

Managing money effectively is emphasised in Islam because several cultural, psychological, and societal money blocks are prevalent within Muslim communities. These notions, whether conscious or subconscious, prevent anyone from achieving the desired level of financial success. The majority of us, as Muslims, face common money roadblocks that prevent us from succeeding in our financial endeavours. Let's talk about them now.

Cultural and Societal Influences on Money Mindset

These influences are not based on Islamic teachings but may arise from cultural norms, expectations, or societal pressures that determine your expectations around money and your conduct. These act as a greater barrier than a physical block, which you may find easy to lift if it's in front of you. To alter your programming, you must be committed.

Let's have a look at a few very common cultural and societal influences that can act as money blocks in Muslim communities:

Cultural emphasis on generosity and family obligations

Maintaining a high degree of generosity and providing financial help to extended family members are strongly expected from a person who acts as an earning family member. This may instil a sense of duty to provide the money even when doing so could jeopardise one's own financial security.

The family is the most essential pillar of Islamic civilisation, and raising healthy children requires extended families. Muslim households typically have huge families that include up to three generations. This offers protection and assistance, particularly during uncertain times. Age is a source of respect because wisdom and experience are linked to a longer lifespan. Taking care of family is regarded as a divine chance.

While supporting family members and being generous to them is considered important in Islam, we, as Muslims, have a duty to fulfil our obligations towards our family, but not to the point of hardship. Islam always favours moderation and prioritises financial responsibilities, such as providing for immediate family and saving for future needs.

Fear of community judgment

In close-knit Muslim communities, individuals may fear being judged for pursuing wealth or investing in new ventures. "Those who own money are selfish," one could think. This is a typical wrong message that a lot of us were taught as children. We believe this message to be entirely truthful. It keeps us back since we don't want to appear egotistical and avoid doing anything that will increase our financial situation. Concerns exist that being too financially ambitious may be seen as materialistic or that one's faith may be questioned if they are perceived as overly focused on money.

Poverty as a symbol of piety

In Muslim culture, poverty is romanticised as a symbol of spiritual purity or closeness to Allah (SWT). Sometimes, this acts as a belief that accumulating wealth is inherently unspiritual or that striving for financial success is at odds with being devout.

This frequently happens because we hear our parents or other influential people criticise wealthy people. Subconsciously, we then take on this financial obstacle and take action to prevent earning additional money. In this context, we are undermining our chances of achieving financial freedom by deceiving ourselves. We might convince ourselves that earning money isn't important.

"I don't deserve to be wealthy."

This lack mentality holds that you're not worthy, fortunate, or intelligent enough to be affluent. It stems from a low sense of self-worth and makes pursuing wealth difficult as you don't believe you deserve it.

Internalised beliefs about wealth, success, and abundance

More traits than large feet, a particular colour in the eyes, self-control, a love of athletics, or an artistic inclination are inherited from parents and grandparents. The majority of us adopt the financial beliefs and attitudes of our families.

Money beliefs, like great-grandma's quilts, family lore, and old photos, are frequently inherited from one generation to the next. To make better financial decisions and experience less financial stress in your life, you may need to start by recognising the beliefs or attitudes that your family has always had about money. In Islam, this concept is closely tied to spiritual beliefs and values. Internalised beliefs, when faced with imbalance, start acting as "money blocks" for Muslims.

Money barriers are unfavourable subliminal thoughts about money that prevent you from fulfilling your consciously held goals. The primary cause of the difficulty in implementing behavioural modifications is the area of the brain involved. Because of the subconscious and conscious parts of our brain, we are stuck in routine.

Our brains are at the theta wave stage for the first five years of our life, during which time they are like sponges, ready to absorb anything and everything. We acquire the skill of personhood by taking everything literally. We learn about all the feelings and emotions around us throughout these initial, crucial five years, leading to the development of habits. Growing up, we were inadvertently instilled with fears by adults. If our parents didn't overcome their irrational fear, it usually trickled down to us, their offspring.

In actuality, we are in charge of how our wealth might work to our advantage and benefit others. Everybody has potential from birth, and it is our natural right to aim high. Words help us create our plans, and our minds have a way of translating them into reality. Our imaginations begin constructing a scenario to defend ourselves since they are designed to keep us safe.

In addition to this, when we grow as Muslims, we may start fearing that the desire to earn more money than we need could lead us away from Allah (SWT), making us greedy or corrupt. This limiting belief can create an aversion to financial success, acting as a block to economic growth.

Asceticism (Zuhd) is often misunderstood as a complete renunciation of worldly pleasures, leading some to avoid wealth out of fear it contradicts piety. Living simply is a means of transcending the material existence and abstaining from worldly wants and the material aspects of life. It is also defined as intellectual indifference to worldly riches and hedonism.

Islam has provided us with guidelines on how to restrain human impulses by following the proper legal precedents and regulations. Islam has also defined guidelines for people to work towards satisfying their souls rather than their bodies to please their Creator. Zuhd does not mean rejecting wealth but rather having wealth without being attached to it. One can be wealthy while practising humility and generosity.

Moreover, sometimes Muslims accept financial struggle as their fate without making efforts to improve their financial situation.

> *The Prophet Muhammad (PBUH) said, "Tie your camel and trust in Allah (SWT)" (Tirmidhi)*

This means a person must make practical efforts and trust in God, rather than assuming destiny alone will determine their financial state.

Reaching financial success might lead to a paradox because of the difficulties, standards, and habits you'll have to give up. This will make your new reality seem foreign and unaccepted. First-generation trailblazers frequently feel like "nothing can be this good" and dread losing everything.

They may also be responsible for ensuring the financial well-being of their friends, family, and community. When someone struggles with guilt due to internalised cultural standards, values, expectations, or emotions of survivor's remorse, the idea of setting clear financial boundaries may seem alien.

Individuals who have financial difficulties frequently have unfavourable thoughts about money. This makes sense—it's easy to become enraged with money when it seems to be in the way of everything. It can become apparent that you despise money when it becomes an ongoing source of stress. However, consider that. The things we detest are typically avoided. How can you ever hope to acquire more money if you despise it? First, you must alter your perspective to improve your financial circumstances.

Understanding the Root Causes of Money Blocks

A vital component of both our personal and professional lives is money. Yes, every financial choice we make greatly influences our well-being. But as Muslims, we still find it challenging to make wise financial decisions, even in the face of a wealth of information and financial guidance. However, how and precisely why do we make financial choices? The psychology of money, or how our attitudes and convictions impact and guide our financial activity, holds the key to the solution. More financial prosperity can be attained by improving our understanding of our connection with money and using that knowledge to make healthier and more educated financial decisions. Let's examine some facets of money psychology and how they impact our financial choices.

Psychological Factors Affecting Financial Attitudes

Achieving financial success requires understanding the complex relationship between psychological and financial action. Financial decisions are not always made purely based on reason; cognitive biases and ingrained emotional emotions also frequently play a role. More efficient money management techniques can be achieved by acknowledging the psychological and emotional barriers that influence financial decisions. Let's explore some key contributors:

The abundance and scarcity mentality

Plenty versus scarcity mindsets is one of the most intriguing ideas in money psychology. What precisely are these mentalities, and how do they influence the way we make financial decisions? The focus of the scarcity mindset is on our lack of certain things. It is well known that those who adopt this mentality fear insufficiency. These individuals put urgent requirements and short-term gains ahead of long-term considerations.

Suppose you have a scarcity mindset and receive an unexpected bonus or another financial windfall. The sudden influx of money can encourage you to squander it all before it disappears. The scarcity mindset makes you prioritise your current demands, which may be helpful in the short term but may not be the best course of action when long-term financial security is considered.

For example, if someone grew up in an environment where money was scarce or viewed as a source of stress, they may develop a scarcity mindset. Alternatively, if one's upbringing emphasised the worldly pursuit of wealth or used money as a tool for status and power, one may struggle with greed or an unhealthy attachment to wealth. In Islam, wealth is considered a trust (Amanah) from Allah, and believers are encouraged to use their wealth responsibly without allowing it to corrupt their hearts.

The abundant perspective, on the other hand, is more focused on what we already have. People who have this kind of thinking feel abundant, full of possibilities, and appreciative of what they already have. They typically have longer-term objectives and a future orientation rather than short-term ones. The mindsets of abundance and scarcity have different effects on our financial choices. These mentalities indeed exist, but they are flexible and subject to change. You can attempt to create a mindset consistent with your values when you know how you feel about money.

> *In the Quran, Allah (SWT) says: "Indeed, your Lord extends provision for whom He wills and restricts it. Verily, He is ever, of His servants, Aware and seeing" (Quran 17:30)*

This verse highlights the concept that wealth and provision are ultimately from Allah, which ties into the idea of avoiding the scarcity mindset by trusting in Allah's (SWT) provision.

Role of limiting beliefs

Subconscious monetary belief systems known as "money blocks" have the power to impede your ability to succeed and prosper financially. These ideas frequently influence our attitudes and actions around money in ways that can be extremely constrictive, all while operating outside of our conscious awareness.

A limiting belief is an idea, stereotype, or generalisation you have come to believe about the world, other people, or yourself. Limiting beliefs can be compared to ship anchors in that they prevent us from navigating the wide range of alternative options and possibilities by locking us into a single, fixed perspective of the world and ourselves.

In Islam, financial success is not inherently sinful; however, a common misunderstanding is the belief that being wealthy is at odds with spirituality. This belief can create a psychological barrier, preventing Muslims from embracing financial prosperity.

> *"And seek the home of the Hereafter with what Allah has given you, but do not forget your share of the world. And do good as Allah has done good to you. And desire not corruption in the land. Indeed, Allah does not like corrupters." (Quran 28:77)*

This verse encourages Muslims to balance spiritual and financial responsibilities, reinforcing that wealth is not inherently in conflict with spirituality.

Emotions' influence on financial decisions

Our financial decisions are typically influenced more by our feelings than by reason. When feelings take precedence over reason, we may make unwise financial decisions. Fear is one of the most common emotions that influence our financial decisions. However, what makes us feel afraid? It could be brought on by losing our jobs, a bad economy, or the worry that we'll miss out on a profitable investment. Fear makes us more likely to act impulsively and make decisions we may regret, like selling stocks too soon or staying away from investments entirely.

Another feeling that affects our financial decisions is happiness. Feeling excited and hopeful about our financial future can lead us to overspending or incurring unnecessary debt. These are among the greatest hazards to achieving financial success. Another emotion that influences many of our financial decisions is greed. Greed can emerge in a variety of ways, such as taking up undue risk or seeking a speedy payoff. Any time greed takes control, it could make us put short-term gains ahead of stability and security in the long run.

It's important to remember that not all emotions negatively influence financial decisions. Feelings of appreciation or satisfaction might influence our decision-making to make more accountable financial decisions, including setting aside money or cutting back on wasteful spending.

Islamic Teachings on Financial Literacy

According to Islam, people are endowed with wealth, which they should manage for the good of human society, even if it belongs to God. According to such guidelines, managing one's wealth is a process that includes creating, accumulating, purifying, preserving, and distributing wealth. It must be done so with caution and in accordance with the law. Let's examine a logical framework that outlines the proper way to handle wealth in accordance with Islamic teachings.

Financial literacy, or the ability to manage money sensibly, is a personal obligation for Muslims. Helping our families and those in need in our community may satisfy our commitments to Allah (SWT) by ensuring that their needs are met and their well-being supported.

A person's ability to manage their finances is crucial to their life and affects many facets of their well-being. Financial literacy has even more meaning in Islam since it instructs us on how to manage our resources wisely and have a beneficial influence on other people.

Financial literacy significantly impacts our lives, especially those of those closest to us. It is essential to our capacity to handle money wisely, make wise choices, and build a secure life for ourselves and those we care about.

Islam places a strong focus on managing our wealth in a fair, considerate, and balanced manner. We should make the most of it to appreciate and enjoy the gifts and privileges that Allah (SWT) has bestowed upon us, but not to the point where we become wasteful or greedy.

The notion of personal accountability in Islam encompasses a wide range of areas, including the way we handle our finances and assets. Every individual bears responsibility for their financial choices and deeds, and Islamic teachings firmly establish this accountability.

> *As Allah (SWT) says in the Quran: "And those who, when they spend, do so not excessively or sparingly but are ever, between that, [justly] moderate." (Quran 25:67)*

This passage from the Quran serves as a helpful reminder to handle money sensibly, avoid extremes, and locate a middle ground that enables us to provide for our families, communities, as well as ourselves.

Furthermore, we are reminded of our obligation to uphold the rights of our loved ones and the underprivileged by assisting them. By doing this, we contribute to the effort to create a future in which our community can prosper and carry on inspiring the next generation.

In turn, Allah (SWT) also states, "And gives the relative his right, and [also] the poor and the traveller, and do not spend wastefully." (Quran 17:26)

Accepting our duty to manage our money might enable us to use it to support others and make wise financial decisions. By encouraging knowledge about finances, we accomplish our own objectives and encourage others to follow suit, sharing information and fostering community growth.

To sum up, financial literacy is very important in Islam since it is consistent with our values of accountability, responsibility, and kindness. When we manage our wealth sensibly, we fulfil our own obligations and improve the well-being of our communities and families.

Hence, money blocks are not merely external obstacles but are often rooted in deep-seated psychological beliefs and past experiences. For Muslims, these blocks can be incredibly complex due to misunderstandings about wealth and spirituality.

By addressing these money blocks through a combination of self-awareness, Islamic teachings, and practical steps, Muslims can improve their financial well-being and align their wealth with their faith, using it as a tool for personal growth and communal benefit.

Chapter Four

Overcoming Fear and Scarcity Mindset

Islamic Perspective on Overcoming Fear and Scarcity

Money mindsets influence how individuals invest, save, and spend their money. However, many people don't realise their perspective on money until later in life. One mindset that can be detrimental is scarcity or the dread of running out of things.

This idea may have originated from various sources, including past financial difficulties, social and cultural pressures, or living in a low-income household as a child. A money mindset, however, is merely a thought pattern that may be altered rather than necessarily reflecting reality. Realising the state of your finances is frequently the first step towards analysing your money perspective.

Scarcity vs abundance mindsets

A scarcity mindset is typified by the conviction that one's resources are finite and inadequate. It causes people to concentrate more on what they lack than what they have, which frequently results in worry, tension, and a persistent feeling that they are short on resources. A scarcity mindset when it comes to money can lead someone to overwork, deprive themselves of necessities, or believe they are unable to save money for the future.

Conversely, those who have an abundant mindset think there are plenty of resources and opportunities accessible, and they could concentrate on opportunity, development, and thankfulness.

This kind of thinking can promote greater adaptability, teamwork, and a readiness to make wise choices and accept measured risks, especially when it comes to money.

There will be many people who think between these two categories. However, transitioning from a deeply embedded scarcity attitude to an abundance mindset requires a mental shift towards a more upbeat and accepting outlook. This could significantly affect your financial security.

Similarly, in the Islamic perspective, the scarcity mindset, often tied to fear of poverty, convinces people that resources are limited and financial security is fragile. This mindset can lead to harmful financial behaviours, such as excessive hoarding, reluctance to spend or invest, and a general distrust in one's economic future.

However, Islamic teachings encourage Muslims to put their trust in Allah's (SWT) provision (Tawakkul) and instruct them to work hard and strive for financial stability.

Our reality is shaped by our thoughts, particularly when it comes to money. The good news is that changing these constrictive money ideas is possible. Through recognition and determination, you may unlock your own potential, which will lead to financial prosperity.

Based on Islamic teachings, here are the ways you can overcome these situations. Let's take a look at them:

Quranic teachings on trust in Allah's (SWT) provision

As Muslims, our steadfast and unwavering faith in Allah (SWT) is the most essential and fundamental aspect of our faith. Thus, we acknowledge that everything we have or shall have in this life and the next is a gift from Allah (SWT). As soon as we acknowledge that Allah (SWT) is the source of all good and bad in our lives, we can begin to embrace the central idea of Islam, which is our complete dependence on Him for all our actions. In Islam, the idea of total reliance or dependence on Allah (SWT) is referred to as Tawakkul.

Tawakkul is essentially "trust and reliance on Allah (SWT)," which means accepting the outcomes that He determines, no matter how they may pan out. In our lives, we will inevitably encounter obstacles and trying circumstances, but we must rise to the occasion with a firm faith in Allah (SWT). Ultimately, Tawakkul is the mindset and belief about entrusting Allah (SWT) with all of our life's concerns.

> *"And He will provide him from (sources) he never could imagine. And whosoever puts his trust in Allah, and then He will suffice him. Verily, Allah will accomplish his purpose. Indeed, Allah has set a measure for all things."* (Quran 65:3)

Tawakkul provides comfort and satisfaction because it acknowledges that Allah (SWT) controls everything. It increases tolerance and perseverance in trying circumstances by fortifying one's faith and dependence on Allah's (SWT) promises. Tawakkul also promotes humility and thankfulness since it helps believers realise how dependent they are on Allah's (SWT) gifts and mercy.

Allah (SWT) makes it abundantly evident in the Holy Quran that Tawakkul is a must and not an option.

> *It says, "...And put your trust in Allah (SWT) if you are believers indeed" (Quran 5:23)*

When we discuss Tawakkul, we mean that we rely on Allah (SWT) and depend on Him for everything. Whether it is about Deen or worldly matters, we rely on Allah (SWT).

Seeking Rizq necessitates having faith in Allah (SWT) and His intentions. The combination of diligent labour and total faith in Allah (SWT) guarantees the unexpected provision of sustenance.

> *"If you were to rely upon Allah (SWT) with the reliance He is due, you would be provided for like the birds: they go out hungry in the morning and return full in the evening." (Tirmidhi)*

Islam's notion of Tawakkul, or having total faith in Allah's (SWT) plan and provision, is closely linked to conquering fear and scarcity. Islam teaches that Al-Razzaq, the Provider, is Allah (SWT). He is the source of all provision, including health, money, and sustenance. This understanding helps believers overcome money concerns, knowing that Allah has already predetermined their provision, and all they have to do is work and have faith in His wisdom.

Fear of poverty, failure, or uncertainty is a natural human emotion. Islam encourages believers to replace this fear with faith in Allah's plan. Allah (SWT) reminds us in the Quran:

> *"And whoever fears Allah—He will make for him a way out and will provide for him from where he does not expect. And whoever relies upon Allah—then He is sufficient for him..." (Quran, 65:2-3)*

Believers are urged to believe Allah (SWT) will always care for them, even in difficult times. This faith diminishes fear because it reaffirms that Allah's (SWT) support is constant.

From an Islamic perspective, fear and scarcity are overcome through Tawakkul—complete reliance on Allah's (SWT) wisdom and provision. By cultivating trust in Allah's (SWT) care, taking action, and being patient and content, a believer can navigate life's uncertainties with inner peace and confidence that Allah (SWT) is always sufficient.

Prophetic examples of resilience and faith in times of financial uncertainty

It is important to emphasise some of the unwavering trials and tribulations that our Prophet (PBUH) endured and, more significantly, his response in such circumstances to understand the essence of knowledge in building resilience while preserving the beauty of our relationship with Allah (SWT).

In numerous prophetic narratives, patience (Sabr) is associated with anticipating an award from Allah (SWT). This implies that paying attention to the benefits Allah (SWT) has promised to His believing people is one way to get through adversity. This will help you see the broader picture and see past your current problems.

In the life of Prophet Muhammad (PBUH), there are numerous examples of patience, resilience and faith during times of financial uncertainty. His approach, rooted in a deep trust in Allah (SWT), provides timeless lessons for facing hardship. Here are a few significant examples:

Though best known for his spiritual counsel, Prophet Muhammad (PBUH) also taught business problems. His life is an example of responsible money management and moral business practices. He showed incredible insight and offered timeless counsel that holds true in today's complicated economic environment.

Muslims have faced a variety of restrictions since the rise of Islam, including economic sanctions that were blatantly against all humanist principles.

However, through wise leadership and making some smart decisions, the Prophet Muhammad (PBUH) was able to navigate Mecca and Medina's difficult financial situations. Initially, he emphasised the importance of self-sufficiency, persistence, and patience. Subsequently, he proposed laws that fostered initiatives, investments, actions, and productivity.

Although he was well-known for leading a modest life, Prophet Muhammad (PBUH) had access to resources. He set an example of contentment and disengagement from material possessions by practising moderation and simplicity. His philosophy on wealth was to spend it prudently for the good of oneself and others rather than to amass it unnecessarily.

> *Holy Prophet (PBUH) advised: "The upper hand is better than the lower hand (i.e., he who gives in charity is better than him who takes it). One should start giving first to his dependents." (Sahih Bukhari)*

The Example of Abu Huraira (RA)

One of the close companions of the Prophet (PBUH), Abu Huraira (RA), experienced severe poverty during his early years in Medina. Despite his dire financial situation, Abu Huraira remained committed to learning from the Prophet and spreading the message of Islam.

His patience and faith during times of poverty were rewarded later in life when he became one of the wealthiest and most respected scholars of his time.

Prophet Muhammad's (PBUH) life offers profound lessons on resilience and faith in the face of financial uncertainty. His reliance on Allah, simplicity in lifestyle, and deep spiritual conviction helped him and his followers navigate periods of economic hardship. These examples encourage believers to maintain their faith, work hard, and trust that Allah's wisdom and provision are always sufficient, even in the most challenging times.

Strategies for Cultivating an Abundance Mindset

The scarcity perspective tells us that whatever we desire in life must come at someone else's expense since there are only so many nice things in the world. It prioritises hoarding over-sharing and rivalry over teamwork. According to the scarcity worldview, things are "the way they are" and accurately reflect the limitations that the outside world presents.

However, looking more closely, we discover that shortage is more frequently artificial than natural. It's a widespread kind of conditioning that teaches us to view the world as inadequate. Thankfully, there is another way to look at things and focus on all the gifts and opportunities around us. A transformational way of thinking about life that can increase your level of contentment, happiness, and peace of mind is the abundant mindset. Here are some strategies rooted in Islamic teachings:

Adopting positive affirmations based on Quranic principles

Making positive remarks about oneself to overcome limiting ideas, confront negative self-talk, and boost self-esteem is known as positive affirmation practice, a type of self-care. Consider making it a regular habit to say affirmations to yourself in the mirror, such as "I am enough," "I love myself," or "I am grateful for the things in my life."

A type of Barakah is the abundant mindset. Will you live an extra year, for instance, if you volunteer your time for a worthy cause? It is true that there is no way to assess the plenty of time in your life empirically, but Barakah is abundance Allah (SWT) has given us that is invisible.

With Allah's (SWT) permission, your time, however limited, will be more fruitful.

When you embody the concept of abundance, you reaffirm and recognise Allah (SWT) as the Only One. He is the only source of fame, fortune, power, and knowledge. He is also the only one who can provide these things. To invite abundance into your life, make a conscious effort to affirm Allah's wonderful names, the Asma-ul-Husna.

Your environment will constantly remind you of them and surround you with positive energy, creating an atmosphere of abundance in your life. This will happen when your eyes often read them, your hands write them, and your ears continuously hear them.

Affirmation: "Allah (SWT) is my Provider, and He will provide for me from sources I cannot imagine." This reminds you that sustenance and abundance are in Allah's (SWT) hands. Trusting His plan helps alleviate anxiety over resources.

> *"And whoever fears Allah (SWT)... He will provide for him from where he does not expect." (Quran 65:2-3)*

Shifting your viewpoint to concentrate on the larger picture might result in a positive transformation. It's easy to let a negative experience send your head into a tailspin when you view it from a narrow viewpoint. Ignoring the little things is simpler when you focus on the broader picture.

Practising gratitude (Shukr) and contentment (Qana'ah) in financial matters

Our tendency to focus on what we lack rather than what we have is one trait that keeps us mired in a scarcity mindset. Focusing on appreciation helps shift the scales back in the opposite direction, focusing your energy on the abundance that already prevails in your life.

As you cultivate gratitude, your joy in the things you have will naturally grow. This practice enables you to start from a place of abundance rather than lack and insufficiency, laying the groundwork for an abundant mindset.

Hence, one of the main themes of Islamic teachings is gratitude. Muslims are instructed to express gratitude to Allah (SWT) for all of life's benefits, no matter how minor. Gratitude is a mindset that can improve our mental, bodily, and spiritual well-being in addition to being a feeling. In Islam, plenty is directly associated with the idea of thankfulness.

We draw additional benefits into our lives when we express gratitude for what we already have. This is so that we might receive more of the things we want since demonstrating gratitude opens our brains and hearts. Being grateful for our blessings makes us more conscious of the wonderful things in our environment, which draws more good things our way.

> *Allah (SWT) says: "If you are grateful, I will surely increase you [in favour]." (Quran 14:7)*

This verse clearly demonstrates that gratitude increases one's gratitude and one's favour with Allah (SWT). Acknowledging your blessings creates space for more abundance in your life, as gratitude is a key principle of attracting better.

Moreover, by recognising that real wealth comes from contentment, you create a mindset of abundance regardless of material possessions. For example, "I am content with what Allah (SWT) has given me. My true wealth lies in my connection to Him."

Being content doesn't mean having everything we want; it means maximising the things we currently have and learning to love them. We experience contentment and serenity when we are happy with Allah's (SWT) plan. Our priorities change from constantly pursuing more material goods to pursuing intimacy with Allah (SWT) and His pleasure.

> *"Richness is not having many possessions, but richness is being content with oneself."* (Sahih Bukhari)

Hence, the concept of wealth and the response to the question "What is abundance?" vary from person to person. Having riches extends beyond material possessions. It refers to possessing the means to live the life you choose. For some people, it's money. For others, it's time to spend with family or pursuing a hobby.

It's not necessary to ignore the effects of financial security in your life in order to have an abundance attitude. It's more important to set constructive goals rather than pursue a large salary because you feel like you should. Adopting a millionaire mindset may change your attitude and accomplish realistic yet exciting goals.

Chapter Five

Developing a Proactive Money Mindset

Shifting from Reactive to Proactive Financial Decision-Making

The term "money mindset" describes your attitudes and ideas towards money and how they influence the way you make financial decisions. This way of thinking has a significant impact on your financial management, influencing actions like investing, budgeting, and debt management.

While a negative money mindset can result in bad financial decisions and more stress, a good money mindset promotes financial stability and progress. Your fundamental views about money typically influence your financial decisions, which can help or hurt your ability to achieve financial success.

If you know how your financial habits and mentality are related, you can start making more deliberate and educated decisions. A positive outlook on money is essential to attaining both financial and personal success. It's a proactive strategy that can significantly impact your capacity to make wise financial decisions; it's not just wishful thinking. When presented with options and obstacles, we employ two different strategies: proactive decision-making and reactive decision-making. Making wise decisions that result in good things requires understanding the distinction between the two.

Making proactive decisions entails foreseeing problems, evaluating the information at hand, and developing plans to deal with them before they even arise. Planning, proactive thinking, and foresight are necessary for this strategy. By being proactive, businesses reduce risks, take advantage of opportunities, and remain ahead of the curve.

Reactive decision-making, conversely, is defined as reacting to events as they happen without much preparation or forethought. It entails making choices in reaction to current events or outside influences. This method frequently results in temporary fixes rather than long-term solutions, even though it might be required in some urgent or unforeseen circumstances. Effective problem-solving and strategic thinking require understanding the differences between proactive and reactive decision-making.

Taking responsibility for financial well-being in accordance with Islamic teachings

Taking responsibility for financial well-being in accordance with Islamic teachings involves adhering to principles of fairness, justice, and ethical conduct, with a strong focus on responsibility towards oneself, family, and the broader community. Key elements include:

Earning a Halal (Lawful) income

The Quran and the teachings of the Holy Prophet (PBUH) both make reference to the crucial idea of earning halal income, emphasising its importance in the Islamic religion. Halal income emphasises the value of upholding ethical and moral principles in financial dealings by referring to earnings or profits obtained by acceptable and permitted means under Islamic law. In Islam, it is crucial to ensure that one's money is derived legitimately and in accordance with Sharia law, which upholds the fundamental principles of honesty, justice, and integrity. The Islamic way of life is based on this idea, which ensures that all money dealings advance individual spiritual development and the well-being of society.

Islam is a way of life that covers every facet of a person's day-to-day behaviour. It offers direction to Muslims on everything from religious deeds to daily interactions.

To ensure our funds are halal, we must first comprehend the fundamentals of halal money. The word "halal," which denotes legal or acceptable, refers to our source of income as well as foods and beverages. In fact, one of the most significant aspects of Islam is the attainment of halal revenue. It is also illegal to spend money acquired by unethical means, such as stealing or earning interest.

There is a close relationship between Islamic finance concepts and the halal money principles. Understanding Islamic finance principles is important before diving into the savings guidelines. Financial systems as a whole are crucial to the distribution of resources because they mobilise savings and household finances and direct them towards investments or productive uses.

This is carried out in line with Sharia in an Islamic financial system. It is also value-oriented since advancing social well-being and achieving socioeconomic justice are just as vital as maximising profits. The following are the fundamental tenets of Islamic finance:

- The primary source of information is Sharia or Islamic law.
- Riba prohibition (interest).
- Prohibition of gharar, or ambiguity.
- Prohibition of gambling, or maysir.
- Prohibition of prohibited objects.

The fact that halal income encourages financial security and stability is one of the key reasons it is so significant in Islam. When individuals obtain their income through methods permitted by Islamic law, they feel secure knowing that their finances are aligned with their spiritual values and beliefs. This assurance allows them to focus on other areas of their lives–such as relationships, personal development, and spiritual growth– by reducing stress and worry tied to financial concerns.

In Islam, halal income is particularly important because it promotes economic security, justice, and stability while leading people to Jannat (Paradise), which is every Muslim's ultimate goal. Following Islamic law when making money enables people to match their financial actions with their core principles and beliefs, giving them a sense of self-assurance and direction. This practice embodies the core of Islamic teachings by promoting individual ethical life and the prosperity and well-being of the community.

The Prophet (PBUH) said: "Avoid the seven destructive sins: associating partners with Allah (SWT) (shirk), magic, killing a person whose killing Allah (SWT) has made unlawful except for a just cause, consuming the property of an orphan, consuming usury, fleeing on the day of the battlefield, and slandering chaste, believing women who are unaware." (Sahih Bukhari)

One of the "seven destructive sins" that Muslims should abstain from, according to this hadith, is usury. It highlights the significance of obtaining one's wealth by morally and legally acceptable means and abstaining from actions forbidden by Islam.

Muslims should focus on achieving material prosperity and spiritual fulfilment by prioritising halal income. This ensures that their financial decisions reflect their dedication to living a life defined by their convictions of justice and morality.

Avoiding Riba (Interest)

The Arabic word "Riba," which means "to increase" or "to exceed," is frequently used to describe exorbitant interest rates on loans. Islamic law forbids charging interest on loans because it is considered Riba or an unfair and exploitative gain. In Islamic banking, Riba refers to charged interest. It's also known as usury or charging exorbitant interest rates.

To maintain fairness in trade, Sharia law forbids Riba. Islam seeks to promote almsgiving and doing good deeds for others. It forbids acting out of self-serving and selfish motivations, which can breed mistrust, resentment, and societal hostility.

The fundamental issue with Riba is that it is unfair to one of the two participants in a commercial transaction or loss from the outset. Muslims believe that interest rates are intrinsically unfair, regardless of the situation, for both the lender and the recipient. Riba is commonly translated as usury, an unnecessarily high interest rate.

Muslims believe that interest-based transactions do not lead to an equitable income split since an unreasonably low interest rate would also put the lender at risk of losing money. Such transactions are inherently harmful to one party or the other and resemble gambling, which is forbidden in Islam.

The practice of riba is a serious evil in Islam, and those who do it risk going to war with Allah (SWT) and His Messenger (PBUH).

> *"O believers! Fear Allah (SWT), and give up outstanding interest if you are true believers. If you do not, then beware of a war with Allah (SWT) and His Messenger! But if you repent, you may retain your principal—neither inflicting nor suffering harm." (Quran 2:278-279)*

Interest is a form of exploitation that benefits the wealthy at the expense of the poor. It enables affluent people to profit assuredly by virtue of their preexisting riches. It punishes the underprivileged whose labour is misused. Since the poor bear all the danger, it is unfair. Paying interest makes it harder for those in poverty to accumulate wealth, often trapping them in a cycle of debt.

Moreover, the penalties associated with most interest-based items, such as overdraft fees and late repayment penalties, exacerbate this. These sanctions worsen inequality by punishing the poor disproportionately.

Avoiding excessive debt

Islam advises against incurring unnecessary debt, especially debts that can lead to financial hardship or dependency. If borrowing is necessary, it should be done with the intention and plan of repayment. Islam supports the forgiveness or easing of debts for those who cannot repay them.

The role of charity

Giving is essential to an Islamic economy in full bloom. Zakat is a required charitable donation, one of our five pillars. This system's beauty is that philanthropy benefits both the giver and the recipient. Giving money away with the proper aim fosters gratitude, empathy, and compassion.

Muslims are urged to freely donate to charity (Sadaqah) in addition to Zakat. Generosity is believed to grow and purify one's wealth rather than reduce it. Giving away money we have earned can serve as a shield against materialism and conceit, two detrimental effects of prosperity.

By applying these principles to our financial lives, we may better ourselves, our loved ones, and society at large. We will also be more successful in the hereafter and feel more content and fulfilled. Regardless of one's religious background, these guidelines are also helpful for anyone looking for a more ethical and holistic approach to personal economics.

Thus, the Prophet (PBUH) advised against using downward social comparisons to prevent the scarcity attitude, which breeds stinginess, and to foster gratitude for one's blessings. As Muslims, we are reminded that wealth is a test from Allah and should not be coveted, and we are cautioned against using the affluent as a benchmark for comparison.

Islamic personal finance teachings provide a thorough and well-rounded approach to wealth management that fosters both monetary success and spiritual development. We are instructed to view wealth from an Islamic viewpoint, concentrating on halal income and moral expenditure, prioritising charity, seeking Barakah, and striking a balance between material and spiritual goals. It is possible to build wealth and wholesome relationships on faith.

Fundamentals of Islamic Financial Planning

Embarking on a Sharia-compliant financial journey involves a thoughtful approach grounded in Islamic values. This process is not just about managing wealth but also about aligning financial decisions with ethical and religious principles.

Islamic financial planning aims to achieve personal well-being while upholding the teachings of Islam, encouraging individual growth and supporting the wider community.

Building a Sharia-compliant financial plan

Creating a Sharia-compliant financial plan requires careful consideration of income, budgeting, and fulfilling religious obligations like Zakat. The goal is to maintain a balanced and ethical approach to financial management, ensuring all activities adhere to Islamic law. Essential components include:

- Ensuring all income is halal (permissible)
- Directing funds towards essential needs and ethical ventures
- Setting aside a portion for Zakat (obligatory charity) and voluntary sadaqah (charity)
- Steering clear of riba (interest) in investments and transactions

Setting Financial Goals in Line with Islamic Values

When establishing financial objectives, it's important to ensure they align with Islamic ethical standards. This involves:

- Supporting the well-being of the community
- Contributing to charitable causes
- Practising mindful consumption
- Pursuing socially responsible investments that promote positive change

Laying out a clear path to meeting Islamic financial goals and a comprehensive, Sharia-compliant financial strategy can enhance individuals' material wealth and spiritual fulfilment.

Embracing Accountability and Stewardship

The Islamic concepts of stewardship (Amanah) are deeply ingrained in the rich fabric of Islamic doctrine. These tenets provide direction, lighting the way for accountable and conscientious behaviour. They remind us of the special duty that Allah (SWT) has bestowed upon us. This obligation requires our whole focus since it is a sacred trust and a duty. We must make prudent use of the resources Allah (SWT) has entrusted us for the good of all. We have to realise that whatever we do affects the environment around us.

Amanah highlights in Islamic teachings that everything in creation is the property of Allah (SWT) and that we are entrusted with its maintenance. In Islam, being a steward involves managing all facets of our lives, not simply the material ones. This encompasses the environment, time, knowledge, and our connections.

> *"Indeed, We offered the trust to the heavens and the Earth and the mountains, but they [all] declined to bear it, being fearful of it. But humanity assumed it, for they are truly wrongful to themselves and ignorant of the consequences." (Quran 33:72)*

Islam's teachings on stewardship and amanah direct us to be reliable in all our interactions, whether with our families, our communities, or the corporate world. It entails being truthful and forthright, honouring our word, and protecting people's privacy. We have been given by Allah (SWT); thus, we ought to use it sensibly and properly. Amanah, for Muslims, is being truthful, devoted, and equitable in all we do. It goes beyond simply keeping our word.

> *"[Remember] when your Lord said to the angels, "I am going to place a successive [human] authority on earth." They asked [Allah Almighty], "Will you place in it someone who will spread corruption there and shed blood while we glorify Your praises and proclaim Your holiness?" Allah (SWT) responded, "I know what you do not know." (Quran 2:30)*

This verse reminds us of Amanah's great faith in us. It is our duty as Earth's guardians, or Khalifah, to preserve harmony and balance in the world. Hence, Amanah represents the idea of being entrusted with something valuable and being accountable for managing it with integrity. When applied to wealth, this concept emphasises the duty to handle resources responsibly and ethically when applied to wealth.

Role of Integrity and Trustworthiness in Managing Wealth

In Islamic teachings, managing personal finance is not merely a matter of wealth accumulation but a reflection of one's faith and ethical responsibility. Central to this perspective is the emphasis on integrity and trustworthiness, foundational principles in Islamic finance. These values guide individual financial behaviour and ensure societal welfare, justice, and equity.

Adhering to these principles is a means for Muslims to align their financial actions with their spiritual beliefs, ultimately leading to both material success and divine reward. Let's explore the role of integrity and trustworthiness in managing personal finance according to Islamic principles and the broader importance of ethical conduct in business and financial transactions.

The concept of integrity in Islamic Finance

Integrity is a key moral attribute that Muslims, in particular, should apply in their daily lives. It also alludes to ethics, a daily concept that is adhered to. The sum of a person's personality traits makes up their character, and it is this quality that drives a person to refrain from actions that can lead to them being viewed as dishonest. A person lacking integrity will exhibit traits such as deceit, betrayal, deviation, corruption, money politics, and similar behaviours. These traits could be prevented by dressing with symbols of integrity like Al-Sidq (honesty).

Integrity's etymology relates to one of its oldest meanings. The word integrity originates from the Latin term "integrity," which means completeness or unit. It implies being complete, whole, unaltered, sound, true, or trustworthy. In essence, integrity is synonymous with honesty.

When someone is honest and acts according to strong moral principles and values, they display integrity.

From an Islamic standpoint, qualities such as trustworthiness, honesty, faith, strong belief, noble demeanour, and power of character can all be directly and concurrently linked to integrity. For believers, following Allah's (SWT) instructions and abstaining from forbidden actions constitutes piety, which is integrity in the highest sense.

Living with integrity means upholding your morals regardless of the circumstances or the number of people observing. It means honouring your particular commitments and abiding by your moral principles. Strong morals or ideals and abiding by them in your words and deeds are characteristics of a person with integrity.

Integrity can be easily conceptualised as the consistent state of one's actions and words. Someone would be lacking in integrity, for instance, if they claimed that honesty was one of their principles but then acted dishonestly or withheld information from others. If honesty is one of your moral values, you'll overcome obstacles by being open and honest with people.

Financial integrity is a vital component of both personal and professional financial management. It entails adhering to moral standards and candour in financial dealings, as well as managing financial matters in a fair, transparent, and accountable manner.

> *Allah (SWT) says in the Quran: "And give full measure when you measure, and weigh with an even balance. That is the best (way) and best in result." (Quran 17:35)*

This verse encourages fairness in transactions, ensuring honesty and transparency in business and personal financial matters.

Simply put, having financial integrity implies that all your financial transactions are honest and open. The consistency of one's behaviours and principles concerning money matters is the essence of financial integrity. By following sound financial principles, you can be sure that all of your transactions—from significant purchases to regular outlays of cash—reflect honesty and justice.

> *"He who deceives is not of us."(Sahih Muslim)*

Deception in financial dealings is strictly forbidden, promoting transaction transparency and fairness.

Being trustworthy is essential to having sound financial practices. In both personal and professional relationships, financial integrity serves as the cornerstone upon which trust is constructed. From a wider angle, maintaining financial integrity involves abiding by the law and encouraging a morally responsible culture.

A person or organisation with solid financial integrity would refrain from dishonest activities that damage the reputation and can have negative legal and social ramifications, like filing false financial reports or taking unethical cost-cutting tactics.

Integrity, from an Islamic perspective in the realm of personal finance, means being honest and truthful in all dealings. It requires an inner commitment to live and speak truthfully. It does not imply perfection but rather a readiness to own up to mistakes and shortcomings as soon as possible and make amends whenever possible.

Having integrity doesn't make one superior to others. It involves respecting people by communicating clearly and keeping your word. Regularly seek input to assess your strengths and areas for growth. Integrity means staying motivated by a genuine desire to uphold morality, even in the face of expense or inconvenience. Integrity is known to be tested during times of crisis.

Moreover, trustworthiness, or Amana in Arabic, is a key virtue in Islam, and it is often mentioned in the Quran and the sayings of the Prophet Muhammad (PBUH). Trustworthiness in managing personal finance has several critical dimensions. The Quran emphasises the importance of fulfilling trusts and contracts:

> *"Indeed, Allah (SWT) commands you to render trusts to whom they are due..." (Quran 4:58)*

When a person enters into any financial arrangement, such as borrowing money, signing a lease, or investing with others, they are bound by the trust they've accepted. Breaching this trust is an ethical failure and a violation of Islamic principles.

A person must refrain from misleading others in any financial dealings. This is particularly relevant today, where misleading advertising, false claims, or hidden fees are common. A trustworthy individual will continually provide full and accurate information, ensuring that all parties clearly understand the transaction.

If someone entrusts you with their wealth—whether through a business partnership, loan or as an investment manager—you are obligated to protect that wealth as if it were your own. Misusing or squandering someone else's money is a breach of trust and a major sin in Islam.

Importance of Ethical Conduct in Business and Financial Transactions

Islamic teachings, which strongly emphasise social duty, fairness, and honesty, are the foundation of Islamic business and trade ethics. These guidelines are intended to promote moral responsibility and the general welfare and assure honest and open company operations.

Muslims have long been involved in business, and Islam strongly supports it as a way to raise living standards and supply material luxuries.

Let's examine the fundamentals of Islamic business ethics, including the function of intention, forbidden behaviours, the value of reliability, and the virtues of humility and charity.

Islamic normative principles form the foundation of Islamic business ethics. These rules are not only suggestions; rather, they are regarded as divine mandates that all Muslims should follow in their commercial transactions. To uphold moral behaviour in business, the core concepts of fairness, honesty, and public good are crucial.

Ethical conduct in business and financial transactions is fundamental to Islamic economic principles. It promotes fairness, honesty, and social welfare. Islam advocates for social justice, ensuring wealth is distributed equitably and avoiding exploitation through prohibitions like Riba (interest).

Ethical behaviour fosters economic stability by building trust and reducing the need for regulation. Those who uphold these standards achieve a positive reputation and long-term success, attracting clients and partners. For Muslims, ethical conduct also means fulfilling spiritual and moral duties, aligning with Quranic values and bringing blessings (Barakah) into one's wealth and life beyond material success.

The role of integrity and trustworthiness in managing personal finance according to Islamic principles cannot be overstated. These values guide every aspect of financial behaviour—from earning and spending to investing and giving. By adhering to these principles, Muslims fulfil their religious obligations and contribute to a more just and ethical financial system.

In a world where greed and dishonesty often seem prevalent, the Islamic approach to finance offers a path to both spiritual and material success based on trust, responsibility, and fairness.

Chapter Six

Islamic Perspective on Earning Halal Income

Importance of Earning Halal (Lawful) Income

Even though our time here on Earth is brief, it is crucial for each of us. As soon as we enter this world, we become aware of many things in our environment. From our experiences and observations, we pick up knowledge along the way.

When we reflect, we come to understand that we truly had no choice but to enter this planet. Furthermore, we were not given the opportunity to be born into a certain family or environment. We had no choice over the features and appearance we were born with. As a result, we conclude that everything that has been formed around us is outside of our control.

We understand that the Lord of all creations is none other but Allah (SWT), the One and Only Creator.

This is the voice of our conscience telling us that everything was made for a reason and a purpose and that everything is subject to the will of Allah (SWT).

WEALTH WITH FAITH

> *"To Allah belongs the dominion of the heavens and the earth; He creates what He wills. He gives to whom He wills female [children], and He gives to whom He wills males."* (Quran 42:49)

This verse emphasises that the circumstances of our birth, including our family and environment, are determined by Allah's (SWT) will.

All things are under the care of Allah (SWT). The real King is him. Therefore, it is imperative that we accurately discern what most pleases Him and what enrages Him. We have to protect ourselves from His fury. In addition to the basic nature and intelligence of humans providing us with the ability to choose the correct path, Allah (SWT) has directed us via the verses of the Quran. We all enter this planet with different sets of abilities. We have many plans and objectives as we expand. In the Quran, it says:

> *"And it is He who has made you successors upon the earth and has raised some of you above others in degrees [of rank] that He may try you through what He has given you. Indeed, your Lord is swift in penalty; but indeed, He is Forgiving and Merciful."* (Quran 6:165)

Thanks to Allah (SWT), man has the capacity for free will. We must understand that this freedom of choice has boundaries and is not unrestricted. While we have the freedom to choose, it's crucial to understand that this is Amanah (a trust that must be returned), so we should only follow His wishes.

How we use the resources and opportunities given to us determines our success, not just in this world but in the Hereafter. Choosing a path that ensures our income is lawful and earned with integrity is one of the most crucial aspects of life.

> *The Prophet Muhammad (PBUH) emphasised the importance of earning Halal income when he said: "The best income is that which a man earns with his own hands and from honest trading." (Sahih Bukhari)*

This teaching reinforces that success is not merely about the quantity of wealth but its quality—how it is earned and the blessing it brings. When we seek halal earnings, we ensure that our wealth is blessed and beneficial for ourselves, our families, and the community at large. It also brings peace of mind and soul, knowing that we are living in accordance with Allah's (SWT) commandments.

Quranic injunctions and Hadith emphasising lawful earnings (Rizq)

Earning a halal (lawful) income is not only a religious obligation but also brings many tangible and spiritual benefits. These benefits go beyond material wealth, extending to a person's peace of mind, blessings in their life, and success in the Hereafter. Here are some key benefits of earning a halal income:

Means of attaining Allah's (SWT) pleasure

The primary advantage of earning halal is that Allah (SWT) will be pleased with the deed. Our Lord is the one we answer to and are to stand before Him. The right way to earn forms the foundation for His happiness. It becomes a vehicle for Barakah and Allah's (SWT) mercy. In the Quran, Allah (SWT) states:

> *"And if only the people of the cities had believed and feared Allah (SWT), We would have opened upon them blessings from the heaven and the earth; but they denied*

[the messengers], so we seized them for what they were earning." (Quran 7:96)

We discover that embracing Iman and Taqwa, which result in abstaining from the forbidden and remaining within the boundaries of acceptable lifestyles, becomes a means of obtaining Allah's (SWT) kindness and opens doors to virtue. Not only that, but it also serves as a foundation for a guy to gain honour and respect. A portion of the hadith refers to it:

> *The Prophet (PBUH) said: "The lawful is clear and the unlawful is clear, and between the two of them are doubtful matters about which many people do not know. Thus, he who avoids doubtful matters clears himself in regard to his religion and his honour, and he who falls into doubtful matters will fall into the unlawful..."*
> *(Sahih Bukhari & Muslim)*

Promotion of justice and fairness

Another factor contributing to its significance in Islam is that halal income supports justice and fairness. When people obtain their income using methods permitted by Islamic law, they may be sure they are not engaging in behaviours that damage or exploit others. This can enhance the general prosperity and well-being of the community and help build a more just and equitable society.

Ways to achieve calm and serenity

Refraining from haram and limiting one's earnings to halal only results in a life of repentance. When people consistently make righteous choices, they experience the sweetness of life and embark on the path to Jannah. Such individuals who choose purity will have their souls taken by angels with kindness and grace. They were the ones who exercised caution in their behaviour, incomes, eating habits, and clothing choices.

The stability of finances

Promoting financial stability and security is a primary factor behind the significance of halal income in Islam. Those who obtain their income in a way that complies with Islamic law can rest easy knowing that their financial matters are taken care of and that their profits are being spent in a manner that aligns with their religious principles. This can lessen tension and anxiety and free people up to concentrate on other facets of their lives, such as their relationships, spiritual development, and personal progress.

Enhanced productivity and progress

Halal income motivates individuals and businesses to operate ethically and with integrity, which fosters long-term growth and success. It leads to greater productivity, as the focus is on honest work and providing genuine value to clients or customers, contributing positively to the economy and society.

In conclusion, earning a halal income is essential for achieving a life that is blessed, fulfilling, and in harmony with the teachings of Islam. It safeguards one's spiritual, mental, and physical well-being, ensuring both worldly success and eternal rewards in the Hereafter.

Avoiding Prohibited Sources of Income (e.g., Riba, gambling)

Income obtained by means that are forbidden by Islamic law is known as haram money. This includes earnings from gambling, interest (Riba), and the selling of goods that are prohibited, such as pork or alcohol. In Islam, it is a grave sin to earn or spend haram money; followers are advised to look for halal substitutes instead.

A person who earns from prohibited sources of income will lose respect and honour if they give in to misgivings that push them towards haram. They will become embarrassed and misguided as a result. Over time, they may lose the ability to distinguish between right and wrong and stray from the righteous path, becoming desensitised to sin and its consequences.

Such a person enjoys no enjoyment, calm, or tranquillity. Despite the wealth that surrounds them, they lead a troubled and unhappy life surrounded by paranoia and anxiety. This is the outcome of their decision to abandon halal and go with haram as a source of income.

What are some examples of haram income in Islam?

Usury (Riba)

Riba, often referred to as usury, refers to an unfair, exploitative relationship created by trade. Two common examples of usury are the unjustified curiosity derived from the repayment of an advance or the concurrent exchange of unequal commodities. The maxim states that one's efforts should not be associated with hoarding wealth and that it is important to take an interest in the risk of losing wealth and growing it through every financial transaction. That is why Islamic law forbids engaging in riba or fascination.

> *The Prophet (PBUH) cursed the one who accepts usury (riba), the one who gives it, the one who records it, and the two witnesses to it, saying: "They are all the same. (Sahih Muslim)*

Making money and lying

One of the greatest transgressions in Islam is deceiving customers by presenting goods at a lower price than their actual value, particularly when there is a shortage of that item.

> *"And do not consume one another's wealth unjustly or send it [in bribery] to the rulers in order that [they might aid] you [to] consume a portion of the wealth of the people in sin, while you know [it is unlawful]." (Quran 2:188)*

Among the most devastating effects of this sin are open belief misfortune and financial debasement. A common example of applying temporary fixes is when employees lack the moral integrity to carry out their responsibilities and obligations. As a result, the income they earn is haram.

Bribery

> *Prophet Muhammad (PBUH) has said: "The worst unlawful earning is the income a governor gains through bribery." (Ibn Majah)*

When a small percentage of people bribe to get what they want quickly, those who refuse to bribe for any reason will face many obstacles in their quest for entitlements. Furthermore, absent payment means the bribe collectors will not fulfil their legal obligations. Therefore, if bribery becomes more widespread among people in society, especially government officials, it will undoubtedly cause a rise in depravity.

Gambling

Furthermore, the money won via betting is haram. This is because Islam strongly encourages obtaining employment through useful vocations and supports working hard and aiming to make money rather than becoming wealthy or losing all of one's money at once.

> *"O you who have believed, indeed, intoxicants, gambling, [sacrificing on] stone alters [to other than Allah (SWT)], and divining arrows are but defilement from the work of Satan, so avoid it that you may be successful."* (Quran 5:90)

Dealing in Prohibited Items

Income from selling or facilitating the sale of haram items, such as alcohol, pork, or any form of intoxicants, is forbidden.

> *"The Holy Prophet (PBUH) said: 'Allah has cursed wine, the one who drinks it, the one who serves it, the one who sells it, the one who buys it, the one who presses it, the one for whom it is pressed, the one who carries it and the one to whom it is carried.'"* (Sahih Bukhari)

Islamic teachings emphasise the importance of ethical, just, and fair earnings. Muslims are encouraged to seek halal (lawful) income through legitimate means and avoid earnings that lead to harm, exploitation, or injustice to others.

Ethical Business Practices According to Islamic Principles

Business ethics transcend laws and norms, emphasising accountability, justice, and honesty. They unify ethics and profits, fostering an environment where businesses strive to achieve greater goals. Islamic business ethics influence how Muslims do business by fusing morality and practicality. These principles, based on the Quran, Hadith, and Sharia law, place an emphasis on social duty, justice, and honesty.

Upholding fairness, transparency, and social responsibility in business

In Islam, upholding fairness, transparency, and social responsibility in business is not only encouraged but considered essential. These values align with key Islamic principles and are integral to maintaining ethical conduct. Here's how they relate to Islamic teachings:

Fairness (Al-'Adl)

"Al-'Adl," or justice, is one of the core tenets of Islam. The Quran and Hadiths reiterate the principles of justice, equity, and fairness regarding all spheres of society, including business. This principle calls for fairness to everyone—clients, business partners, and working men alike. The idea that riches and wealth originate from Allah (SWT) and that humans are merely His stewards is the foundation for the demand for fairness in business.

> *"Indeed, Allah commands you to render trusts to whom they are due and when you judge between people to judge with justice." (Quran 4:58)*

This verse underscores the importance of honesty and fairness in all dealings. It speaks directly to the need for justice in business, encouraging ethical behaviour where no party is wronged.

Business fairness refers to a transaction in which no party should be cheated, exploited, or granted any unequal terms of exchange. For instance, both the buyer and seller are rightly attributed. The seller should give the commodity or service at a fair price without overcharging and inflating it unethically. Similarly, the buyer shall pay a reasonable price without attempting to take undue advantage of the seller.

Fair treatment of employees is always emphasised in Islam. Therefore, employers are reminded to provide just wages, humane conditions of work, and scope for professional development. Underpayment or exploitation of workers is absolutely prohibited. Again, not only money but the dignity and respect given to employees have a hand in the business process.

> *The Prophet (PBUH) also said, "Give the worker his wages before his sweat dries." (Sahih Al-Bukhari)*

This hadith stresses the importance of prompt and fair payment to workers, reinforcing the idea that exploitation or delaying compensation is a grave injustice in Islam.

Similarly, Islam disapproves of holding up necessary commodities to create price inflation (Ihtikar) and related financial manipulations like acquiring excessive interest from loans (Riba). These are considered unjust because they create an undue burden on others, specifically those in needy circumstances. The mission is to ensure that the business transaction is undertaken not to harm anyone or imbalance society.

In this light, the principle of justice in Islam covers a Muslim's personal, economic, and social behaviour. It urges honesty, openness, and respect for different dimensions, resulting in justice in all matters, big or small. The words of the Quran and Hadith remind Muslims to act justly, as their wealth and actions must benefit society.

Transparency (As-Sidq)

As-Sidq in Islamic business ethics relates closely to honesty, truthfulness, and transparency. For this reason, Islam insists that buying and selling transactions be communicated in the straightest manner so they are not misinterpreted or misconstrued to cause friction. All business transactions must be devoid of misleading information, fraud, or deception; therefore, both parties should know exactly what is expected of them.

> *"And do not mix the truth with falsehood or conceal the truth while you know it."* This verse highlights the prohibition of concealing the truth in any dealings, emphasising the need for openness and honesty in business transactions. *(Quran 2:42)*

Transparency refers to disclosure, wherein a seller is supposed to communicate about or inform about every necessity concerning the product or service offered for sale, the defect, or the weakness, in order to make an informed decision on the part of the buyer. Failure to disclose such information or false declarative aspects for purposes of sales involves unethical and, by extension, haram acts prohibited in Islam.

> *The Prophet Muhammad (PBUH) said, "The truthful merchant [is rewarded as] the Prophet, the truthful, and the martyr." (Tirmidhi)*

This hadith raises the social standing in accordance with those who engage in business with fairness and sincerity and offers them high rewards in the Hereafter. It depicts how highly Islam values champions and the extent to which it holds transparency as a significant marker in ethical business practice.

> *The Prophet Muhammad (PBUH) said, "The seller and the buyer have the right to keep or return goods as long as they have not parted; and if they spoke the truth and made clear the defects of the goods, then they would be*

blessed in their transaction, and if they told lies or hid something, then the blessings of their transaction would be lost." (Sahih Bukhari)

This hadith emphasises the blessings associated with honest and transparent dealings, as well as the negative consequences of deceit or misrepresentation.

Islamic teachings promote the pursuit of transparency in finance, which requires all parties to enter into unambiguous contracts. The contracts should clearly define the parties' rights and obligations and not leave wiggle room or hidden clauses. This makes it clear what every individual is expected to do and avoids creating scope for disputes in the future.

Social Responsibility (Al-Ihsan)

Another key component of Islamic business ethics is social responsibility, known as Al-Ihsan. Apart from doing business justly and transparently, there is a responsibility to positively impact society. Islam encourages the proper sharing of wealth and allows the affluence bestowed upon a person to support those in need, aligning personal success with the greater good of social welfare.

The Islamic practice of Zakat, which obliges Muslims to donate a percentage of their money to the less fortunate, is intimately associated with social responsibility. By redistributing wealth, Zakat helps to support the most vulnerable sections of society, including the poor, widows, and orphans. This act of compassion is not limited to individuals; companies are also encouraged to participate in charity endeavours and fund projects that benefit the underprivileged.

"Righteousness is not that you turn your faces toward the east or the west, but [true] righteousness is in one who believes in Allah (SWT), the Last Day, the angels,

> *the Book, and the prophets and gives his wealth, in spite of love for it, to relatives, orphans, the needy, the traveller, those who ask [for help], and for freeing slaves."*
> *(Quran 2:177)*

This verse highlights the importance of charity and generosity as central to righteousness, encouraging businesses and individuals to contribute to the welfare of society.

Islam also strongly emphasises the necessity of finding or producing goods and services that do not harm the environment or society. Enterprises are urged to abstain from actions that could lead to over-exploitation or worsen environmental damage. This aligns with the Islamic idea of guardianship (Khilafah), which views humans as custodians of the earth, making environmental protection a fundamental duty.

> *The Prophet (PBUH) also said, "The best of people are those who are most beneficial to others." (Sahih Bukhari)*

It is, therefore, legitimate to state that the values of justice, openness, and social responsibility are fundamental to Islamic business ethics. The problem is that adhering to these values is essential for preserving society's overall well-being and performing or carrying out economic operations fairly and ethically.

First, fairness dictates that everyone in a transaction gets what they deserve, and transparency states that all transactions are honest and transparent. Businesses that practise social responsibility put society before their own interests by actively improving it. By putting these ideas into practice, people and businesses may create a successful market while also upholding Islamic principles of justice, integrity, and compassion.

Supporting Halal Economy and Ethical Entrepreneurship

A growing movement favouring the halal economy and ethical entrepreneurship links financial activities to moral precepts drawn from Islamic teachings regarding sustainability, justice, and social responsibility. The term "halal economy" describes any economy sector that adheres to Islamic law, including food, finance, fashion, and tourism. However, the ethical underpinnings that consumers cherish—transparency, sustainability, and justice—make them appealing to audiences outside of the Muslim community.

Ethical entrepreneurship is characterised by the embodiment of values like integrity, honesty, and social responsibility. Here, the entrepreneurs prioritise the bottom line and the health of their staff, clientele, and community. They adhere to Islamic financial principles that condemn riba and promote risk-sharing while avoiding exploitative, environmentally damaging, or oppressive labour practices.

This, in turn, creates higher levels of inclusiveness and diversity in global markets. With the increased demand for halal products and services, companies see a great opportunity to serve their customers better through higher ethical standards. This economy promotes fair trade practices and ethical sourcing; conversely, it persuades businesses to contribute to social welfare and create a sense of prosperity for their communities.

Endorsing the halal economy can help create an ecosystem that balances economic growth with moral and ethical issues. It encourages ethical business conduct that is consistent with universal principles of justice, equity, and sustainability, as well as faith-based values, fostering a more moral and just global economy.

Chapter Seven

Budgeting and Financial Planning in Islam

Concept of Budgeting and Financial Discipline

Regardless of one's religious views, budgeting is an essential component of personal finance. It includes keeping tabs on earnings and outlays, establishing financial objectives, and making future plans.

A carefully thought-out budget can assist people in reaching financial stability, avoiding debt, saving for emergencies, and making smarter financial decisions.

Islamic personal finance is a distinct money management strategy in line with Islamic values. Making and saving money is not the only thing at stake; another is ensuring that all financial transactions adhere to Islamic law (Sharia) and are carried out ethically. This includes avoiding interest (Riba), generating income through halal (permissible) ways, and donating a portion of one's wealth through charity giving (Zakat).

Budgeting assumes much greater importance in the context of Islamic personal finance. In line with Islamic principles, it serves as a tool for managing finances and a way to exercise self-control, accountability, and fairness in financial dealings.

Muslims can ensure that their financial actions align with their beliefs and lead wealthy, moral, and balanced lives by practising good budgeting. Let's have a look in detail!

Prophetic Guidance on Moderation and Avoiding Extravagance (Israf)

Islam strongly emphasises moderation, and this idea extends to money matters as well. Muslims are suggested to abstain from Tabdhir (wasteful spending) and Israf (extravagance).

This is not to say that Muslims should forgo material comforts or live in poverty. Instead, individuals are urged to live simply but pleasantly and refrain from making needless or extravagant purchases.

Islam forbids both extravagant living and miserliness. Life is a test for everyone, and wealth–described in the Quran as fitna—is one of the many ways through which Allah, the Exalted, tests humanity.

> *Allah (SWT) says: "Your riches and your children are merely a trial. And there is a mighty reward in the presence of Allah (SWT)." (Quran 64:15)*

In every situation, wealth is a test, more or less. People can be divided into two main categories:

The first group consists of those who see themselves as self-sufficient and do not believe in Allah (SWT). They contend that they are unrestricted by anyone and free to choose where to spend and how to spend their resources, claiming that their success, riches, and possessions are all the result of their own efforts. These people actually believe they are in charge of their own life and are the disciples of Pharaoh, Qarun, Haman, and others.

The second group believes in Allah (SWT) and holds the belief that all they possess, including their honour, money, and life itself, is a gift from Allah (SWT). They view all these blessings of life as a trust from Allah (SWT), which makes them trustees rather than proprietors. Consequently, they feel obligated to live their lives in accordance with the wishes of their Almighty Master, Allah (SWT), following in the footsteps of the holy Companions. Similarly, they firmly believe in Allah (SWT) and kindly spend their income on His path. Thus, they are the cherished and unselfish slaves of Allah (SWT).

Miserliness and generosity are like two rivers running parallel to one another. There aren't many people on the banks of the generous river despite the water being chilly and lovely. These individuals are truly fortunate. On the other hand, the water of the River Miser is tasteless and salty, but there is a large crowd of people both inside and along its banks. These are the misfortunes of the material world.

An action's eligibility for counting towards Israf is determined by evaluating if it goes beyond what is necessary or what the populace generally considers to be within reasonable bounds. A person has acted with Israaf, for instance, if they need a particular amount of clothes but continue to buy more than they need. What is typically seen as normal or excessive determines this.

There will always be a spending cap that most individuals consider appropriate. If you spend more than this, it will be considered extravagant and excessive unless you have a good reason supported by Islamic beliefs.

Another important lesson of the Prophet's (PBUH) guidance is moderate behaviour, according to which extravagance as israf in one's life is not welcomed; this principle is much grounded in the principles of Islam and reflects one of the requirements for having a balanced and meaningful life.

Here are a few specific lessons from the Sunnah and the Quran:

Moderation in consumption

The Prophet (PBUH) taught that excessive consumption, whether in food, wealth, or resources, leads to waste and harm, both spiritually and physically. He emphasised the importance of living moderately.

> *"Eat and drink, but waste not by extravagance. Certainly He (Allah SWT) likes not those who waste by extravagance." (Quran 7:31)*

Simplicity in lifestyle

The Prophet (PBUH) led a simple life despite having access to wealth and resources. He demonstrated how one can live with contentment and gratitude while maintaining a minimalist lifestyle.

> *Anas ibn Malik reported: "The Prophet never ate on a table, nor on small plates, and he never ate soft bread." (Sahih Bukhari)*

Charity and avoiding greed

Islam encourages generosity and the sharing of wealth, but it also warns against using wealth in a wasteful manner that benefits no one. Charity (sadaqah) is encouraged, but extravagance (israf) in spending on luxury and self-indulgence is discouraged.

> *"The son of Adam will not pass away from Allah (SWT) until he is asked about five things: how he lived his life, how he utilised his youth, with what means did he earn his wealth, how did he spend his wealth, and what did he do with his knowledge." (Tirmidhi)*

Balance in worship and worldly affairs

The Prophet Muhammad (PBUH) advised against extremes in worship or worldly matters, urging a balance between both. He cautioned against asceticism that disregards the rights of the body and family while also discouraging excessive indulgence in worldly pleasures.

> He said: *"Verily, your body has a right over you, your eyes have a right over you, and your wife has a right over you." (Sahih Bukhari)*

The prophetic guidance on moderation and avoiding extravagance (israf) serves as a reminder to live a balanced life, use resources wisely, and avoid wastefulness. It encourages contentment, charity, and a mindful approach to consumption, ensuring that wealth and blessings are used to please Allah (SWT) and benefit society.

Developing a Halal budget

A vital first step towards obtaining stability and prosperity is creating a budget and taking financial responsibility on a journey. Budgeting should incorporate values like accountability, justice, and honesty for individuals wishing to harmonise their financial habits with Islamic ideals.

Why is creating a household budget necessary?

You may have heard phrases like "we are on a tight budget these days," "income is not sufficient," and "unable to survive." Certainly, there are a few defenceless persons whose income is so low that, even with their expenses cut, they cannot meet even their most basic necessities. May their circumstances be improved by Allah (SWT)!

Some people, meanwhile, are likewise capable of earning money but lack the knowledge of how to spend it. Recall that it is preferable to plan before you spend money than to regret it afterwards. Thus, we could spare ourselves a lot of anxiety if we create a budget to keep income and expenses in check.

An Islam-based home budget would need to adhere to a few principles in the Quran and Sunnah, such as practising moderation, responsible stewardship, and abstaining from luxury. The following outlines a methodical approach to developing a household budget from an Islamic perspective:

Intention (Niyyah)

Begin by creating a genuine intention to manage your family finances to please Allah (SWT). Be certain that your earnings and expenditures are purely legal and halal. Ensure your wealth is earned and spent in halal (permissible) ways.

> *The Prophet Muhammad (PBUH) said, "Actions are judged by intentions, so each man will have what he intended." (Bukhari & Muslim)*

Assess your income

Determine how much money you and your family make, ensuring it comes from halal sources. This covers income from investments, business earnings, salaries, and any other reliable sources.

Prioritise Zakat and charity

Allocate a portion of your earnings for Zakat, compulsory charity, which is 2.5% savings above the nisab threshold. Sadaqah, or regular voluntary charity, is also encouraged in Islam to purify wealth and benefit needy others. The first preference to give is that of family members or relatives in need, as taking care of them forms the essence of Islamic charity.

"They ask you what they should spend. Say, 'Whatever you spend of good is [to be] for parents and relatives....'"
(Quran 2:215)

Classify essential costs

Sort your spending into categories, making sure to moderately and equitably assign priority to necessities:

- Basic needs (Daruriyat): Your top priorities should be food, clothing, shelter, utilities, education, and medical expenses.
- Debts (if applicable): Next, pay off halal debts (like those with no interest).
- Transportation: Allocate for transportation costs while avoiding unnecessary luxury.

Avoid Riba (Interest)

Islam strictly forbids Riba. Avoid giving or taking interest-bearing loans or investments. Pay off your debts with interest as soon as possible.

Plan for savings

Focus on saving for future necessities after attending to your immediate needs. Islam promotes moderation and balance; therefore, it's critical to make plans for things like retirement, marriage, and the education of one's children. Savings are seen as a component of Tawakkul, or having faith in Allah (SWT), but in moderation with accountability.

Budget for wants and emergencies

Set aside a small sum for comforts and non-essential but permissible (halal) indulgences while avoiding israf (extravagance), which is forbidden in Islam. It is in accordance with Islamic principles to spend only what you can afford or to purchase things that promote wastefulness or vanity.

> *The Quran advises: "Indeed, the wasteful are brothers of the devils..." (Quran 17:27)*

Moreover, save for an emergency fund for the unexpected. This prevents future financial constriction or reliance on impermissible means such as borrowing with interest.

Review and adjust

Review your budget regularly and adjust it to your changing needs and conditions. Islam encourages constant self-evaluation and improvement. Keep a record of what's coming in and going out so you keep track of your financial goals in a way that keeps your deeds halal.

> *Allah (SWT) says: "O you who have believed, fear Allah (SWT). And let every soul look to what it has put forth for tomorrow..." (Quran 59:18)*

Manage your home finances in a way that supports both financial and spiritual well-being by basing your budget planning on these concepts.

Practical Tips for Halal Financial Planning

Islamic financial planning is the systematic management of one's finances, adhering to the principles of Sharia. Traditional financial strategies were merged with ethical considerations in asset growth and charitable giving but without forbidden activities. Let's have a look at them!

Strategies for Saving, Investing, and Charitable Giving

If you regularly set aside a certain amount of your monthly income, it will be easy to acquire more financial stability. The secret is to make saving a regular part of your financial routine, regardless of whether you're preparing for unexpected expenses or aiming to purchase a significant item.

Islamic views on savings diverge from those of the majority, who often save their money by depositing it in banks or investing it for personal gain. Muslim ideas of frugal living encompass giving to the poor, advocating for Islamic education in schools, contributing to charitable activities, and helping to build mosques. This is not only a charitable approach; rather, it is an investment in Akirah that will result in enormous benefits from Allah (SWT) that are not yet disclosed.

It encourages us Muslims to handle our money sensibly and refrain from wasting it. There are crucial factors to take into account to ensure our financial habits continue to be consistent with our religion, even though many of the principles of saving money are comparable to traditional approaches.

Let's discuss how to save money quickly as a Muslim, providing you with Islamically compliant methods and pointers to assist you in reaching your financial objectives and securing a better future.

Develop the habit of saving

A small monthly savings can significantly impact your peace of mind and bank account. It can seem overwhelming if you don't devote time to saving consistently, but it doesn't have to be. Setting up a monthly recurring payment into a different savings account is an easy first step.

If you receive a monthly salary, scheduling the transfer for just after payday is a good idea. Your ability to save comfortably may vary depending on your unique situation, but even £50 a month will add up over time without significantly reducing your disposable income.

Acquire financial understanding and budgeting skills

Understanding how to create a successful budget is one of the cornerstones of responsible financial management for Muslims. To begin, take these actions:

- Keep tabs on all of your earnings and outgoings for 30 days.
- Determine whether you're saving money or overspending by comparing your monthly income and expenses.
- Determine variable costs (such as food shopping and entertainment) and fixed costs (such as rent and utilities).
- Determine which variable costs you can reduce to boost your monthly savings.

Pay off debt

The first step to achieving outstanding halal financial freedom is paying off debt. In addition to being costly and having negative emotional effects, debt is one of the primary Islamic duties that every Muslim has to do before passing away. Even though having debt may feel oppressive, you can boost your hard-earned savings and be free of financial debt and worry by following an effective debt payback plan.

Establish an allotted savings account and set up bills and savings automation

Ensure you have a specific savings account to spend your money wisely on everyday expenses. This division reduces the possibility that you may raid your savings to cover unexpected costs, protecting your financial objectives and warding off temptation.

Monitor your finances by automating bill payments and savings contributions. Set up recurring monthly automatic transfers from your daily expenditure account to your savings account. Automating bill payments also helps avoid late fines, which is consistent with managing finances responsibly and on time.

Monitor your expenditures

One of the most important aspects of prudent financial planning that can help you save more is keeping track of your expenses. To keep your wallet safe, decide where to make cost reductions first. Then, make sure you pay attention and maintain your savings goal by using the expenditure tracker app.

Reducing wasteful expenditures is yet another great way to increase your savings. First, decide what your priorities are by figuring out where you can save money, such as by eating out or paying for unnecessary subscriptions. Next, search for options like cash back on purchases or an awards program. Finally, transfer the funds you have saved to your savings account.

Examine and make changes

If your financial situation changes, you might need to adjust your savings strategy. To stay on course, review your aim from time to time and make any required adjustments. In summary, developing better halal-saving practices requires dedication and perseverance. By implementing these tips, you may improve your savings practices throughout the year and accomplish your financial objectives. Recall that every little bit matters. So, get started now and see your savings increase!

Using Islamic Financial Tools For Wealth Management

Islamic financial instruments, such Musharakah and Mudarabah, which are exempt for riba and gharar, have given rise to distinctive wealth management plans based on Sharia principles. These investment approaches are seen as morally righteous.

- **Mudarabah**

A Mudarabah contract is essentially a business partnership contract. To clarify, Mudarabah involves a collaboration in which one partner

WEALTH WITH FAITH

finances an enterprise and the other oversees operations. The investor in a Mudarabah arrangement is known as Rabb-ul-Maal, while the company's manager is known as Mudarib. The investment itself is known as Raas-ul-Maal. In Islamic banking, Mudarabah is frequently used in conjunction with other Islamic monetary agreements to structure bank deposit accounts.

Which kinds of mudarabah are there?

Depending on the company's demands and the degree of control that Raas-ul-Maal desires, the Mudarib can choose between two primary forms of mudarabah contracts for investing and managing capital.

A restricted mudarabah, also known as a Mudarabah Muqayadah, is one in which the Rabb-ul-Maal chooses the kind of business or location for cash allocation. The Mudarib must follow the financier's terms when investing the funds.

In contrast, an unrestricted Mudarabah (Mudarabah Mutlaqah) allows the Rabb-ul-Maal to grant the Mudarib complete discretion over how to use the cash, with little to no constraints other than ensuring that the investment complies with Sharia.

While the Mudarib is empowered to make business decisions under this agreement, significant financial decisions, such as taking out loans or disbursing substantial amounts of money, typically require the approval of the financier.

Application in Wealth Management

Mudarabah is commonly used in investment funds or savings accounts. Banks or investment firms manage the capital investors provide in Sharia-compliant ventures, generating profits. This allows capital holders to grow their wealth while avoiding interest-based systems.

Example: Islamic banks offer Mudarabah-based savings accounts, in which depositors (Rabb-ul-Maal) earn a share of profits based on the bank's investments in approved sectors.

- **Musharakah**

In Islamic finance, a Musharakah is a joint venture or partnership structure wherein stakeholders split an enterprise's gains and losses. While Sharia, the Islamic legal code, forbids making money from interest on loans, Musharakah permits a project's or business's financier to obtain a return in the form of a predetermined percentage of the real earnings. In contrast to a traditional lender, the financier will also participate, pro rata, in any losses that may arise. In Arabic, shirkah Al-amwal, or collaboration, is known as "sharing." Musharakah is one kind of this.

Different Musharakah Types

There are many cooperation arrangements within Musharakah.

- **Shirkah Al-'Inan:** a relationship in which one partner acts just as the other's agent and provides no further guarantee.

- **Shirkah Al-Mufawadah:** an unconstrained, equal, and limitless partnership in which each partner contributes the same amount and is entitled to the same profits and rights.

- **Permanent Musharakah:** an association that lasts indefinitely until its members elect to discontinue it; frequently utilised to meet long-term financial needs

Application in Wealth Management

It suits real estate investments, business financing, or joint ventures. Wealth managers can invest in Musharakah projects where clients contribute capital, sharing the potential upside and downside, thus providing a balanced approach to risk.

Example: In a Musharakah Mutanaqisah (diminishing partnership) used for home financing, both the client and the bank co-own the property, gradually buying out the bank's share through payments.

Forwards from Islam (Salam and Istisna)

These unique funding options are only available to specific kinds of businesses, and gharar does not apply to them. The item is delivered at a predetermined future date, and the payment is made in advance. The assistance of an Islamic legal expert is typically necessary because these contracts must meet a number of requirements to be deemed genuine.

Renting (Ijarah)

Selling the right to use an item (usufruct) for a set period of time is known as leasing or ijarah. For a lease term, one requirement is that the lessor retain ownership of the leased item.

The ijarah wa 'iqtina variation of the lease stipulates that a written lease must include the lessor's commitment to sell the leased object at the end of the lease for a fixed residual value. Only the lessor is bound by this promise. The lessee is not required to buy the item.

By integrating tools like Mudarabah and Musharakah, Islamic wealth management promotes a holistic, ethical, and socially responsible approach to growing wealth while adhering to Islamic values.

Chapter Eight

Overcoming Debt and Managing Financial Obligations

Islamic Perspective on Debt and Borrowing

One of the biggest obstacles people face while navigating personal finance and entrepreneurship is handling debt and financial commitments. As consumer culture and financialisation continue to dominate the world, debt has become commonplace for many people and countries.

Islam provides insightful guidance on managing debt, advocating prompt repayment and a debt-free lifestyle. In Islam, debt is a severe issue. It is a duty that must not be disregarded or taken lightly. The Quran and Hadith, together with other religious texts, regulate borrowing and debt in Islam.

Borrowing and debt are regarded as a type of interpersonal assistance and collaboration. Given the enormous reward it bears, this deed is highly respected and encouraged.

Many Muslims in this present materialistic society are unaware of what debt is and how it ranks as a problem among the key ones in Islam.

Many Muslims find comfort in living on credit, incurring debt to drown themselves in needless expenses and to seek and maintain a lifestyle that is outside their means and control.

The social and economic fallout from debt in today's societies appears to be so completely numbing too many. They take out loans for incorrect purposes, such as to indulge their whims and fantasies or to achieve instant success, as they imagine their friends to be. They accumulate unmanageable debt and occasionally are forced to use one loan to pay off another, ignoring that death could strike at any time.

In Islam, taking out unneeded loans is a grave offence. After you've consumed all you need, you shouldn't take out a loan unless it's absolutely necessary. It is required of you to have a modest lifestyle devoid of excessive material consumption.

Debt, in terms of money and the economy, has always been a necessary part of human existence. While debt may assist with investment, consumption, and economic progress, it also comes with various hazards and duties for both individuals and society as a whole.

The concept of debt is seen in the Islamic setting not just from an economic perspective but also from an ethical and moral one.

Islam is a comprehensive and all-encompassing religion that provides exact guidance on many aspects of life, such as the morality of debt. The hadiths of the Prophet Muhammad (PBUH) and the Quran offer detailed guidelines for how one should act and behave when managing debt. Moreover, the fundamental principles of Islamic debt ethics are Ihsan (kindness), Amanah (trustworthiness), and Adl (justice).

Sharia strikes the ideal balance. It protects lenders and creditors, offers guidance to both borrowers and debtors and provides counsel for creditors to guide their behaviour. Here are some guidelines on how Sharia strikes a balance between rights and guarantees everyone's rights are respected.

The concept of debt in Islam

Debt is governed by the Islamic concept of Muamalah, which is based on reciprocal assistance (Ta'awun). This implies that debt should not be incurred for personal or commercial gain but rather to assist others in need. Debt is viewed as a kind way to support people who are struggling financially.

Debt is defined by two fundamental terms: Dayn and Qardh. Dayn is a general term that refers to having debt or giving one. It can be used to describe a number of circumstances in which an individual is obliged to repay another. The Quran refers to it, particularly in Surah Al-Baqarah (2:282), whereby the necessity of promptly repaying obligations is emphasised. Dayn can emerge from several scenarios, such as loans or recompense for damages.

However, Qardh particularly designates a kind of loan in which the lender lends part of their money to the borrower in exchange for repayment. In contrast to Dayn, which can stem from various duties, Qardh is solely a giving gesture meant to help those in need. In conclusion, Islamic law requires that debt be repaid, and debt is seen as a means of charitable giving rather than a way to make money.

Islam takes into account societal obligations and the welfare of the group as a whole in addition to individual behaviour. Assisting those in debt is regarded as a good deed that will bring about recompense from Allah (SWT).

> *In one narration, it is declared, "Whoever relieves a believer's distress of the distressful aspects of this world, Allah (SWT) will rescue him from a difficulty of the difficulties of the Hereafter... and whoever alleviates [the situation of] one in dire straits who cannot repay his debt, Allah (SWT) will alleviate his lot in both this world and in the Hereafter." (Sahih Muslim)*

Conditions approved for debt and loans

Debt and borrowing are acceptable in the following circumstances:

- **When necessary:** Borrowing is required when it is essential to meet basic needs.

- **Intention to repay:** The borrower should intend to settle debts to prevent procrastination.

- **Written agreement:** To prevent disputes, there should be witnesses and a formal agreement on the debt. It is taught that one should not pass away in debt.

Thus, Islam sees debt and borrowing as lawful and even recommends that the borrower repay the obligation in the agreed time or as soon as feasible.

Prophetic Guidance on Avoiding Debt and its Consequences

The importance of swiftly repaying debts is underlined throughout the Prophet's (PBUH) teachings. Paying debt is a virtue that leads to Allah's (SWT) pardon and pleasure. It's a means of keeping one's word and behaving honourably. It is also a means of thanking and showing kindness to the creditor who assisted the debtor during his difficult period.

> *The Prophet (PBUH) said, "Whoever takes a loan intending to repay it, Allah (SWT) will help him, and whoever takes a loan intending to waste it, Allah (SWT) will destroy him." (Ibn Majah). He (PBUH) also said, "If anyone remits anything from a debt owed to him, he will have that amount recorded for him as a charity." (Sunah Abu Dawud)*

> *In another hadith, it was reported: "The soul of the believer is suspended because of the debt until it is settled." (Tirmidhi)*

This hadith emphasises the necessity of repayment and the grave consequences of passing away in debt.

> *The Prophet (PBUH) would supplicate to Allah (SWT) to save him from debt. He would say, "O Allah, I seek refuge in You from a soul that does not satisfy and from a heart that does not humble itself and from a supplication not heard and from knowledge that does not benefit and from a deed not raised up and from a debt that never ends." (Musnad Ahmad)*

> *In another narration, the Prophet (PBUH) sought Allah's (SWT) refuge from debt. Abdullah ibn Umar narrates, "When the Prophet contracted a debt transaction, he would say: O Allah, I seek refuge in Thee from care and sorrow, from incapacity and laziness, from stinginess and cowardice, and I seek refuge in Thee from the burden of debt and from being humbled by people." (Abu Dawud)*

Debt in Islam is a serious issue, not just in terms of responsibility and obligation but also in the moral aspect. In fact, Prophet Muhammad's (PBUH) teachings speak much more about the importance of paying off one's debts, worldly issues for the debtors themselves and having spiritual consequences. His dua describes a deep concern for how debt can accumulate in a man's life while also seeking Allah's (SWT) assistance in evading or alleviating the burden of debt.

From various hadiths, we come to know that when an individual has debts paralysing their soul, causing distress, they should intend to repay their obligations while seeking Allah's (SWT) help. On the other hand, those who incur debts to waste or default are destined for ruin.

The Prophet's (PBUH) prayers for deliverance from the burden of debt remind us that financial integrity is not separate from spiritual well-being and that seeking divine help and keeping a good intention to repay is a prerequisite to fulfilling this duty.

Ethical Considerations in Borrowing and Lending Money

In Islam, borrowing and lending have a plethora of legislations founded on principles of equality, justice, and mutual goodwill. These principles, derived from the Quran and Hadith, aim to facilitate ethical financial transactions that benefit both parties and prevent exploitation.

The main rules of borrowing and lending in Islam include:

Prohibition of interest (Riba)

Interest, charging or paying it is strictly prohibited in Islam. Lending should be done without expecting any extra monetary gain. Charging interest is exploitative because it takes advantage of a borrower's needs.

> *Allah (SWT) says in the Quran: "But Allah (SWT) has permitted trade and has forbidden interest." (Quran, 2:275)*

Draughting the agreement

Any lending or borrowing transaction should be documented, especially if substantial sums are involved. The loan amount, terms of repayment, and due dates should all be made very clear in the agreement.

This guarantees that all parties know their responsibilities and helps prevent future problems.

> *"O believers! When you contract a loan for a fixed period of time, commit it to writing. Let the scribe maintain justice between the parties. The scribe should not refuse to write as Allah (SWT) has taught them to write. They will write what the debtor dictates, bearing Allah (SWT) in mind and not defrauding the debt. If the debtor is incompetent, weak, or unable to dictate, let their guardian dictate for them with justice. Call upon two of your men to witness. If two men cannot be found, then one man and two women of your choice will witness—so if one of the women forgets the other may remind her. The witnesses must not refuse when they are summoned. You must not be against writing contracts for a fixed period—whether the sum is small or great. This is more just for you in the sight of Allah (SWT) and more convenient to establish evidence and remove doubts. However, if you conduct an immediate transaction among yourselves, then there is no need for you to record it, but call upon witnesses when a deal is finalised. Let no harm come to the scribe or witnesses. If you do, then you have gravely exceeded your limits. Be mindful of Allah (SWT), for Allah (SWT) is the One Who teaches you. And Allah (SWT) has perfect knowledge of all things." (Quran 2:282)*

This verse states that transactions should ideally be recorded to provide ethical proof and hold on the parties involved. The absence of written documentation in the present era frequently causes problems and gives the parties concerned the ability to argue with one another. This is made possible because one party gains from the deal at the expense of other parties.

Openness and disclosure

When it comes to lending and borrowing, transparency and disclosure are fundamental ethical and Islamic values that guarantee borrowers have access to complete and accurate information regarding loan terms, fees and repayment requirements. Ethical lenders are dedicated to providing clear and transparent information to borrowers, enabling them to make educated financial decisions and understand the risks and costs connected with borrowing money. Openness in lending procedures encourages accountability and trust, strengthening ties between lenders and borrowers and lowering the possibility of misunderstandings or conflicts.

Equity and parity

Ensuring equity and justice in credit and monetary resource access is one of the primary ethical considerations in lending and borrowing. Lending policies should ideally be accessible and non-discriminatory, giving people and businesses the same chances to obtain credit based on their financial needs and creditworthiness rather than characteristics like gender, race, or socioeconomic level. Ethical lenders empower marginalised communities and borrowers who face hardship by giving fair and transparent loan terms in an effort to advance social equality and financial inclusion.

Impact on the environment and society

Beyond the specific transactions involved, lending and borrowing decisions may have wider social and environmental effects. Ethical considerations may cover the evaluation of the environmental and social effects of lending operations, including the financing of initiatives or businesses that promote long-term viability, environmental stewardship, and ethical behaviour. Environmental sustainability, social equality, and business ethics are just a few of the elements that ethical lenders take into account when making lending decisions. They also evaluate these criteria when assessing loan candidates and investment prospects.

Mercy in repayment

If the borrower is genuinely unable to repay the loan on time, the lender is encouraged to show leniency by extending the repayment period or even forgiving the debt if possible. Showing compassion to those in financial difficulty is highly rewarded in Islam, and lenders are urged to avoid pressuring or harassing borrowers.

Avoiding excessive debt

While borrowing is permissible in cases of need, Islam advises against taking on excessive or unnecessary debt. Borrowers should be cautious to avoid putting themselves in situations where they cannot repay their obligations. The Prophet Muhammad (PBUH) cautioned against excessive debt, as it can lead to stress, dishonesty, and an inability to meet other Islamic responsibilities.

Ensuring repayment

Borrowers have an ethical obligation to repay loans on time, as failure to do so without valid reasons is considered a form of dishonesty and oppression. It is essential to keep the trust and fulfill agreements promptly. Those who are able to repay should not delay or default deliberately, as this can harm the lender and society at large.

In sum, Islam encourages lending as an act of charity and social responsibility while ensuring that both borrowers and lenders adhere to principles of fairness, compassion, and justice. Ethical borrowing and lending in Islam aim to foster a more equitable and just society, free from exploitation and oppression.

Strategies for Debt Repayment and Financial Freedom

Achieving financial freedom, particularly when burdened with debt, requires a strategic approach. Here are several effective strategies that can help guide you toward repayment and eventual financial independence:

Implementing Debt Repayment Plans (Qard al-hassan) Based on Islamic Principles

Qard al-hassan is used in Islamic finance to describe interest-free loans. In most cases, the borrower will repay the amount due under the principal amount in a transaction, including Qard al-hassan, without incurring any additional markup or interest payments. Financial products from Qard Al-Hassan comply with Sharia law, which states that paying interest (Riba) is forbidden regardless of the interest rate. If a Muslim wants to borrow money without paying interest, these loans provide a means of doing so.

> *Allah (SWT) says in the Quran: "Establish regular prayer and give regular charity and give Allah (SWT) Qard Hassan." (Quran 73:20)*

Qard al-hassan loans in Islam and Islamic banking are interest-rate-free, allowing both consumers and businesses to borrow money on a goodwill basis. Qard al-hassan loans are typically utilised for welfare reasons. According to the Quran, Muslims should try to lend these kinds of charitable sums of money whenever they can to anyone in need of such services.

Muslims can promote the social justice principles underlying Islamic finance through the Islamic principle of Qard al-hassan. Islamic finance makes it possible for people who have money to lend it to people who don't without violating Sharia law. One way to think of Qard al-hassan is as a kind of lending arrangement similar to charitable giving, where both parties – the lender and the borrower – sign an agreement outlining the terms of the loan.

From a religious standpoint, in Islam, debt management has been given an ethical stance and social responsibility, with Qard al-hassan serving as the principal form of loan. These loans foster community development by encouraging local funding intitiatives, often organized by a local mosque or charity.

Repayment terms have to be flexible and considerate of the borrower's situation, while also incentivising timely repayments. This approach follows the principles of Islamic finance practice and encourages cooperation and mutual aid in the community.

Supplications for Debt Repayment

In Islam, seeking help from Allah (SWT) through supplications (duas) for debt repayment is a common practice. Let's have a look at a few of them!

It's reported that the Prophet Muhammad (PBUH) used to seek refuge from the burden of debt. One supplication he taught is: "O Allah, I seek refuge in you from anxiety and sorrow, from helplessness and laziness, from cowardice and stinginess, and from the burden of debts and the oppression of men."

> *Allah (SWT) says in the Quran: "And if someone is in a difficult circumstance, then [let there be] a postponement until [a time of] ease. And if you give from your surplus, it is best for you." (Quran 2:280)*

Moreover, charity boosts the chances of good blessings while reducing the financial burden imposed. Seeking repentance and forgiveness for past misdeeds can also ward off hardships. Guidance from knowledgeable people or trusted friends, particularly regarding financial assistance, is crucial.

Reckon on Allah's (SWT) wisdom and timing because relief may come unexpectedly. However, sincere efforts to manage and repay debts should accompany these prayers. Only with faith and confidence can Allah's intervention (SWT) be made to solve financial issues.

Chapter Nine

Investing Wisely According to Sharia Principles

Principles of Sharia-Compliant Investing

Investing in compliance with Sharia law is an essential part of Islamic finance. The designation "socially responsible investing" comes from the need to access funds that adhere to Islamic ideals. As charging interest is forbidden, Islamic banks agree to a specific profit or loss from the operation.

Like most others, a Sharia-compliant social investment fund will be concerned with the social impact it creates for recipients as well as the financial return. Additionally, it must abide by Sharia Law, or Islamic law, which mandates that funds of this kind be administered in accordance with the fundamental tenets of Islam.

Social investment, by definition, follows Mudarabah, which divides risk, earnings, and losses among stakeholders. Since both parties bear some risk and are shielded from one party's benefit at the expense of another, risk sharing also advances the Islamic concept of "togetherness."

Sharia-compliant investing is aimed at preventing social harm and safeguarding the individual. For instance, lending money at excessive rates of interest is illegal due to the risks of debt, hyperinflation, and monopolising investment to the advantage of high-end investors.

Understanding investment

Investing is the process of purchasing assets with the hope that their value will rise over time. When the asset's value rises, the investor receives a return in the form of income payments or capital gains. Throughout history, investing has always been linked to wealth accumulation and the desire for capital income. Nonetheless, investing can also be a way to enhance one's and one's community's quality of life.

When you can sell the asset you invest in for a greater price after it appreciates in value, investing becomes profitable. Appreciation occurs when the value of the asset rises. Investing may be risky, complicated, and full of technical challenges. Muslims may find the world of halal investing to be increasingly intimidating when the Sharia laws are taken into account.

Investments and trading that adhere to Sharia law, which is predicated on moral saving and investing principles, are considered Sharia-compliant. Islamic financial and investing concepts are founded on equitable treatment, non-exploitation, and halal investments that result in a win-win collaboration.

What is halal investing?

Halal investing is a type of ethical investing that adheres to Sharia law, which is the way of Islam. Investments that comply with Sharia direct funds towards business endeavours that uphold Islamic values found in the Quran, Hadith, and Sunnah.

The almighty word of Allah (SWT) disclosed to the Prophet Muhammad (PBUH) is known as the Quran. The Sunnah refers to the customs of the Prophet Muhammad (PBUH) and his followers, whereas the Hadith are the assembled sayings of the Prophet (PBUH).

Islam prohibits Muslims from purchasing assets that violate sharia norms. As a result, halal investments are appropriate. The reason for this is that halal investments advance the ideas of ethics and social justice.

In contrast to the secular financial system, Islamic finance places a strong emphasis on partnerships that benefit both parties and socioeconomic justice. Consequently, you will discover that Islamic investments are less risky and promote social responsibility. Islamic belief does not hold that societal well-being and personal financial gain are mutually exclusive. Both can, therefore, should co-exist.

Guidelines for Halal Investment Practices in Islam

There are precise conditions that make an investment halal. This is an inventory of those standards.

Interest or Riba should not be generated by the investment: Muslims are forbidden by Islam from engaging in Riba transactions. In general, Riba means taking a further sum or interest in a financial transaction. This action is against the teachings of Sharia. Muslims are required by Islam to choose investments free of interest or Riba. Therefore, it is advised that Muslims use caution while deciding which investments are halal and which are haram.

The investment must be free from gambling or Maysir: It is not advisable for Muslim investors to engage in gaming. Any kind of asset wagering is forbidden. Maysir, or gambling, can take the form of forecasting or guesswork with a payment need in advance. Islam, therefore, maintains that investing is not a means of Maysir or gambling.

Gharar must be avoided by Muslim investors: A financial investment in Islam has to be devoid of gharar. Gharar is, in general, a hesitancy, deception, or act of injuring others. Because of its ambiguity, gharar could take the shape of a contract that incorporates fraud. Furthermore, gharar can be trading unclearly. To put it another way, for fairness between the parties, the transaction's contract needs to be explicit.

Focus on asset-based

Within the Islamic faith, money is viewed as merely a means of transaction with no inherent worth. Money used for financial gain is forbidden, or haram, in most Islamic countries. Since money should never be invested in, most income-based securities like bonds and money market mutual funds are prohibited.

Investing in assets, like real estate or fine art, focuses on obtaining tangible items with inherent value. The appreciation of an asset's value generates returns on an asset-based investment.

Investing in a small business is also an excellent example of an asset-based investment. Businesses provide goods and services to create value. A company that expands over time gains value and provides investors with either short-term or long-term rewards. Precious metals, stocks, and technology are examples of asset-based investments.

Types of Sharia-Compliant Investments

- **Halal investment choices**

If you're new to halal investing, you might assume that prospects for Sharia-compliant investors are limited. However, that's not the case. Investing in halal can be very flexible. As an ethical investor, you would have a plethora of investment options at your disposal. Carefully checking investment prospects for haram activity is crucial. Here are some halal investment choices for you to consider.

Sharia-compliant bonds: Islamic versions of bonds that aren't debt-based are called sukuks. Sukuks allow investors to earn from corporate profits, while traditional bonds only allow investors to profit from interest. Sukuks invest directly in a company by pooling the funds of several individuals. Rather than earning interest, investors get a set portion of the profits made by the firm via its operations. Investors also get their main amounts returned after the sukuk matures.

Stocks: Acquiring stock enables one to own a portion of ownership in a company. Upon purchasing stock, an investor becomes a shareholder in the business and is eligible to partake in its assets and earnings. Market capitalisation, which is a stock market representation of a company's value, is how stock market investors make money. As long as a company's financial operations and the industry it operates in comply with Islamic law, stocks are deemed halal.

Property: Real estate is a tangible asset with inherent worth that typically increases over time. Acquiring real estate is kosher as long as mortgages with interest aren't used to buy land or real estate. Families and investors wishing to purchase real estate can apply for interest-free mortgage loans from Islamic banking organisations.

For halal investors who would rather take a more hands-off approach to real estate investing, property investment trusts (REITs) are also feasible investment possibilities. Steer clear of mortgage-based REITs and give preference to those who make most of their revenues from rental income.

Crowdfunding: Crowdfunding pools tiny sums of money from multiple people for a certain firm or project. Typically, an internet platform is used to make this kind of investment. Investors acquire equity shares in the business or project in proportion to their contribution. For first-time investors who wish to reduce their risk, crowdfunding makes sense.

Venture capital: Venture capital (VC) investing is available to halal investors with the necessary funds and industry-specific expertise. In exchange for stock, venture capital investors offer money and advice to start-ups, small firms, and medium-sized enterprises. Venture capital investors benefit from the valuation and earnings of businesses as partial owners, which is permissible.

Precious metals and gold: Buying gold and other precious metals is probably one of the oldest and safest investing strategies. Similar to property, these commodities act as a hedge against hyperinflation and are valuable beyond investing goals. As long as precious metals are purchased and sold at a reasonable price, owning and dealing in them is entirely permissible.

- **Haram investment choices**

Certain investment types are obviously prohibited by Islamic law due to the way their profits are made. Investors in halal should avoid the following categories of investments.

Savings accounts: Typically, investors want to create passive income from their investments, so they put money into high-yield savings accounts. The annual percentage yield (APY) of high-yield savings accounts indicates the annual percentage return (APR) you will receive to keep your money in the account. The use of interest in these investment vehicles makes them obviously haram. In some cases, you might not even be aware that the savings account you have is earning money. To avoid this problem, open a savings account in an Islamic banking establishment.

Bonds: Bonds are fixed-rate loans that investors make to governments, businesses, and other entities for a predetermined amount of time. In addition to receiving their principal amount returned at maturity, investors receive periodical interest payments in the meantime. Because interest is the source of investment gains, bonds are seen as haram.

Forex: Online investing in the form of foreign currency trading entails trading currencies on a worldwide, decentralised market. Traders must speculate on the movement of currency exchange rates when they purchase some currencies and sell others at the same time.

Islamic scholars generally hold the opinion that forex trading is prohibited, especially in the retail sector. From a Sharia standpoint, a number of forex trading characteristics cause concern and are challenging to reconcile with the tenets of Islamic finance. Halal investors are, therefore, encouraged to avoid forex trading altogether.

Derivatives: A financial contract known as a derivative has an underlying asset, or set of underlying assets, that establishes its value. Derivatives include futures contracts, swaps, binary options, and forwards. Due to their reliance on making predictions about the future direction of an asset's price, derivatives are regarded as prohibited. According to Islamic law, derivatives carry a great deal of danger, uncertainty, and speculation. They are, therefore, forbidden.

In Islamic finance, Sharia scholars play a crucial role in determining whether investments comply with Islamic principles. These scholars review financial products, company operations, and market strategies to ensure adherence to halal standards. For Muslims seeking investment opportunities, consulting with a qualified Sharia advisor can help make informed, compliant choices. Investing in accordance with Islamic principles requires careful evaluation of where the money is going and how it is being used. The primary aim is to engage in transactions that not only generate profit but also contribute to the welfare of society while avoiding exploitation or harm.

The Power of Diversification in Halal Investing

Investing in a variety of assets, such as stocks, sukuk, and commodities, as opposed to concentrating them in one place, is known as diversification. This strategy lessens the effect that the performance of any one asset will have on the portfolio as a whole. In the long run, a more consistent and maybe larger return can be achieved if one asset outperforms the others.

Diversification is a cornerstone of prudent investing, frequently described as the idea of "not putting all your eggs in one basket." Given the restricted pool of assets available to build a halal portfolio, diversification becomes even more crucial in the realm of halal investment. You may optimise returns and better manage risk by diversifying your investments across different asset classes and markets. That being said, it's crucial that the assets you select adhere to Sharia regulations to maintain halal returns.

For example, assume a scenario when the stock market dips. If all of the stocks in your portfolio are down, your entire investment may suffer. The impact of the stock market's volatility, however, may be mitigated if you have diversified by holding gold and sukuk, protecting your cash and helping you stay on course with your financial objectives.

In Islamic finance, diversification follows principles of risk-sharing and avoiding excessive speculation. A diversified portfolio can include Sharia-compliant stocks, representing companies that adhere to Islamic laws and permissible business activities. Sukuk, or Islamic bonds, offer stable income through partial asset ownership while complying with Sharia principles.

Real estate investment, whether direct or via Sharia-compliant REITs, provides opportunities for capital growth. Commodities like gold and silver are permissible and act as a hedge against inflation. Additionally, Islamic mutual funds and ETFs allow investors to diversify across professionally managed, Sharia-compliant assets, enhancing portfolio stability and ethical alignment.

Key considerations for Islamic investors include conducting due diligence to ensure investments align with Sharia principles, managing risks by evaluating the risk-return profile of each asset, and regularly reviewing the portfolio. Consulting with Islamic scholars or financial advisors is also essential to ensure investment decisions align with Islamic ethics. Ultimately, diversification in Islamic finance helps investors build resilient portfolios that meet both ethical and financial objectives.

Chapter Ten

Generosity and Charity in Wealth Management

Importance of Sadaqah and Zakat

Being generous can help you achieve your strategic financial planning objectives in addition to having a beneficial impact on your community. Giving to charity causes can be a free choice when managing your wealth; in addition, there may be tax benefits associated with charitable giving. See how people may properly manage their wealth and make a difference in the lives of others by learning how to keep more of what you have so that you can contribute more.

A key component of strategic financial planning is resource allocation that supports both your short–and long-term objectives. Contribution plans might be incorporated into this procedure by designating a specific budget or portion of earnings for charitable purposes. Incorporating generosity into your financial strategy allows you to prioritise open-handedness while ensuring that your wealth supports social and personal goals.

It is exactly the faith and practice of Islam that keeps charitable giving at its very heart. This means concepts such as Sadaqah (voluntary charity) and Zakat (obligatory alms) are among the most powerful ways

WEALTH WITH FAITH

to worship, and it is through them that people can purify their riches, help others, and, through all this, become closer to Allah (SWT).

These acts are not only charitable but also social triggers, which dispense justice and equalisation in society, making the values of sympathy, sacrifice, and gratitude more robust. Sadaqah and Zakat are both emphasised vastly in the Quran and in the teachings of Prophet Muhammad (PBUH); they are full of spiritual benefits and promise to have a broader beneficial influence on the lives of the giver and the receiver.

Quranic Injunctions and Prophetic Traditions on Charitable Giving

The Quran repeatedly highlights the significance of giving, encouraging believers to share their wealth with those who are less fortunate.

> *Allah (SWT) says, "The example of those who spend their wealth in the way of Allah (SWT) is like a seed of grain that sprouts seven ears; in every ear there are a hundred grains. And Allah (SWT) multiplies the reward for whom He wills" (Quran 2:261)*

This powerful verse illustrates the exponential reward of charity in this life and the hereafter. Giving for the sake of Allah (SWT) blesses not only one's wealth but also reinforces a person's sense of fulfilment and purpose. As one of the five pillars of Islam, Zakat is recommended and compulsory for those who meet the necessary financial threshold.

> *The Quran states: "And establish prayer and give Zakat, and whatever good you put forward for yourselves—you will find it with Allah (SWT)" (Quran 2:110)*

This verse stresses that paying Zakat is as important as praying daily because it purifies one's wealth as well as becomes a testimony of gratitude for the blessings received from Allah (SWT).

In addition to Zakat, Sadaqah is another extremely important aspect of Muslims' routines. Although Zakat is compulsory and must be paid at a particular time, Sadaqah is issued on a voluntary basis, and a Muslim is at liberty to give it at any point in time without regard to his financial position.

> *The Quran encourages Muslims to be generous, saying, "Who is it that would loan Allah (SWT) a goodly loan so He may multiply it for him many times over? And it is Allah (SWT) who withholds and grants abundance, and to Him, you will be returned" (Quran 2:245)*

Here, Allah (SWT) invites the faithful to give freely, promising them multiplied rewards for their generosity.

The Prophet Muhammad (PBUH) also placed immense importance on giving charity. He once said, "Charity does not decrease wealth", emphasising that charity, instead of reducing one's possessions, brings divine blessings that enhance a person's wealth in both spiritual and material ways. This teaching reflects the Islamic belief that everything one owns ultimately belongs to Allah (SWT), and by sharing it, a person secures Allah's (SWT) blessings.

> *In another hadith, the Prophet (PBUH) said, "The believer's shade on the Day of Resurrection will be his charity." (Tirmidhi)*

According to this Hadith, charity serves as a shield after death, shielding the giver from the heat and tribulations of Doomsday. The Prophet

(PBUH) placed more emphasis on giving than on speaking, which lends credence to the idea that charitable giving serves as both a social duty and a form of protection, encompassing the giver in the kindness and grace of Allah (SWT).

The Prophet Muhammad (PBUH) also advised that even the smallest act of charity, done with sincere intention, is rewarded.

> *He (PBUH) said, "Save yourself from Hellfire even if it is by giving half a date in charity." (Bukhari)*

This demonstrates that no act of kindness is too small in the eyes of Allah (SWT). Whether large or small, every contribution towards helping another is cherished and rewarded.

Benefits of Generosity and its Spiritual Rewards

Generosity is a core virtue in Islam that fosters a connection with others while elevating one's spiritual standing. Giving purifies the heart, freeing it from greed, pride, and attachment to worldly possessions. By sharing wealth, one acknowledges Allah (SWT) as the true provider, deepening trust in His sustenance.

Moreover, charity cleanses one's soul and protects oneself from spiritual ailments.

> *The Quran mentions, "Take from their wealth a charity by which you purify them and cause them to increase (in righteousness)." (Quran 9:103)*

This purification refers not only to the physical wealth but also to the soul of the giver, who becomes more mindful of their blessings and more empathetic toward others.

Generosity also strengthens social cohesion. Zakat, for instance, is an economic safety net for the Muslim Ummah to take good care of the needy, orphans, and others who need special care. Zakat and Sadaqah ensure the distribution of wealth, hence an attempt to reduce economic inequalities and build a just and harmonious society. Charity is a practical application of this love, manifesting concern for other people's welfare.

In addition to benefiting society, charity brings countless personal rewards.

> *It is said in the Quran, "Those who spend their wealth by night and day, secretly and openly, they will have their reward with their Lord. And no fear will there be concerning them, nor will they grieve" (Quran 2:274)*

This promise of reward reflects the inner peace and satisfaction that accompanies selfless giving. Generosity shields the believer from the anxiety and sorrow that often accompany attachment to material possessions, granting them contentment in both this world and the next.

> *In another hadith, the Prophet Muhammad (PBUH) highlighted the ongoing nature of rewards from charitable deeds, saying, "When a man dies, his deeds come to an end except for three: ongoing charity, beneficial knowledge, or a righteous child who prays for him."*

This illustrates how Sadaqah Jariyah—continuous charity, such as building wells, schools, or other beneficial projects—can provide rewards long after a person has passed away, leaving a lasting legacy of good.

Charity in Islam is not merely an act of benevolence but a deeper expression of faith in itself, epitomising compassion, empathy, and responsibility towards others. Zakat and Sadaqah together draw calls among Muslims to be generous and mindful of the needs of communities that create a balanced and equitable society. Spiritual rewards of charity given are immense, as Allah (SWT) promises immediate and eternal benedictions for those who give from the heart. Charity, according to the Quran and the teachings of Prophet Muhammad (PBUH), is not just a social responsibility but also a way to lead a person towards Allah's mercy and enrichment of the soul.

Integrating Charity into Financial Planning

Giving to charity is a moral obligation and a crucial aspect of budgeting in Islam. Muslims are urged to practise wealth mindfulness, which includes setting aside a certain amount of their wealth on a regular basis for charitable causes.

By including Zakat and Sadaqah in their financial plans, Muslims can ensure that their wealth is acquired and spent morally. This would help them balance their material prosperity with spiritual development. This method not only helps the giver but also significantly contributes to uplifting society's less fortunate people by encouraging compassion and unity.

Including charity in financial planning reminds us once again that Allah (SWT) has allowed individuals to treasure their wealth to relieve others in need. However, repeated charity also purifies the wealth further and guards against evil to even attract even more bounty.

As Allah (SWT) says in the Quran, "But whatever thing you spend [in His cause]—He will compensate it, and He is the best of providers" (Quran 34:39)

Thus, when Muslims set aside part of their earnings for charity, they are investing in both their worldly success and their hereafter.

Calculating and Distributing Zakat According to Islamic Guidelines

In addition to being a required charity, Zakat is one of Islam's five pillars. It addresses the required contribution that Muslims, who have reached the nisab, or minimal financial threshold, must make before they're required to pay Zakat. Savings, investments, company assets, and other acceptable types of capital are all included in this wealth. What is the general rule? As a general rule, 2.5% of one's excess wealth that has been possessed for a full lunar year ought to be contributed as Zakat!

Muslims calculate Zakat by listing all their assets, excluding personal commodities like clothing, household goods, and essentials, such as gold, silver, cash, investments, and commercial products. Liabilities, such as debts or any kind of expense, are then subtracted. If the remaining wealth surpasses nisab, 2.5% of the sum must be paid in Zakat. Every year, Islamic institutions or scholars adjust the nisab based on the current price of silver or gold. The threshold is often revised once a year to account for prevailing market conditions and other developments that Islamic organisations or scholars may have identified.

> *In terms of distribution, the Quran explicitly outlines eight categories of recipients for Zakat: "Zakat expenditures are only for the poor, the needy, those employed to collect [Zakat], those whose hearts are to be reconciled [for Islam], to free captives, for those in debt, for the cause of Allah, and for the stranded traveller." (Quran 9:60)*

This ensures that Zakat is allocated to those who are most in need, thus playing a crucial role in reducing economic inequality and helping the most vulnerable members of society.

Zakat computation and distribution are significant acts of worship that go beyond a financial duty. Muslims are reminded of the ephemeral nature of money and the significance of allocating it in a way that advances the community at large as they carry out their Zakat obligation. Giving Zakat fulfils Allah's requirement to help the less fortunate while also cleansing one's riches and keeping it blessed and free from spiritual harm.

Practising Regular Sadaqah to Purify Wealth and Earn Allah's (SWT) Blessings

Sadaqah is a voluntary charitable donation that Muslims are encouraged to make on a regular basis, whereas Zakat is required. In contrast to Zakat, which has set guidelines and is paid annually, Sadaqah is given at any time and in any amount. It can include any act of kindness, such as lending a helpful hand to someone in need, grinning, or giving wise counsel, and is not limited to monetary contributions.

> *The Prophet Muhammad (PBUH) said, "Every act of kindness is charity" (Bukhari)*

Implementing regular Sadaqah in your financial planning is cleansing wealth on a regular basis so that it does not become the root of greediness. In the same manner as one keeps his body healthy through exercising regularly, doing charity cleanses the soul and eliminates attachments to material wealth, such as selfishness or greediness.

Regular Sadaqah has the power to ward off calamities and hardships as well.

The Prophet Muhammad (PBUH) said, "Give charity without delay, for it stands in the way of calamity."
(Tirmidhi)

Providing regular charity earns a Muslim Allah's (PBUH) good pleasure along with protection from worldly and hereafter difficulties. Whatever any individual gives in charity, no matter how small, during the day, Allah (SWT) considers it charity.

Apart from its spiritual advantages, Sadaqah promotes cohesiveness and a sense of community. It inspires Muslims to attend to the needs of others, so reducing poverty and suffering in the community. This kind deed promotes a sense of shared responsibility and deepens the relationships between people. Muslims are reminded of their obligation to care for others through Sadaqah, fostering a society that is more just and compassionate.

Incorporating Zakat and Sadaqah into financial planning is essential to the Islamic way of life. Both forms of charity allow Muslims to purify their wealth, express gratitude for Allah's (SWT) blessings, and support the community. Zakat ensures that a portion of wealth is systematically redistributed to those in need, while Sadaqah provides a continuous opportunity to give and earn Allah's (SWT) pleasure.

Together, they serve as powerful spiritual tools that not only protect wealth but also promote social justice and harmony. By regularly giving both Zakat and Sadaqah, Muslims are reminded of the blessings they have been given. They are encouraged to use their wealth in a way that benefits not only themselves but the wider community.

Chapter Eleven

Building Long-Term Financial Stability

Long-Term Financial Goals and Legacy Planning

In Islam, financial planning extends beyond short-term objectives or immediate needs. One key aspect is wealth preservation, which ensures that assets are safeguarded for future use. Besides wealth preservation, there is also wealth transfer, that is, intergenerational wealth transfer. Lastly, a significant element of this planning is leaving a legacy after death.

Muslims are encouraged to be mindful of how their wealth is to be managed not just during their lifetime but also after death. Setting clear goals for the preservation of wealth and adding an estate plan in conformance with Islamic principles ensures that the distribution of a Muslim's wealth follows the principles of justice and fairness as set down by the Quran and Hadith.

Setting Goals for Wealth Preservation and Intergenerational Wealth Transfer

Preserving wealth over the long term and transferring it in a manner that benefits future generations represents one of the most important aspects of Islamic financial planning. In Islam, saving, investment, and responsible management of wealth are sought among Muslims not only for their self-interest but also for the interest of their progeny. The more detailed branch of this great responsibility of responsible resource management and leaving behind a financial legacy beneficial to generations to come is the planning of inter-generational wealth transfer.

Clear financial goals constitute the beginning of long-term wealth preservation. Such goals include funding children and grandchildren for education, health care, and general well-being, supporting charitable causes, and securing the financial futures of family members. Islamic financial planning promotes prudence and patience, encouraging Muslims to spend modestly and save prudently.

An important aspect of wealth preservation is saving against inflation and other risks, such as economic downturns. In Islam, there are various permissible investments that adhere to ethics, including equity investment, real estate, and profit-sharing arrangements known as Mudarabah and Musharakah. Again, in addition to preserving and growing, they remain permissible as Islamic investments as they avoid interest and unethical business.

Therefore, in planning a transfer of wealth, a Muslim would have to consider the material and spiritual legacy left behind. A well-planned transfer of wealth can ensure that future generations can sustain themselves above and beyond their financial independence and foster a sense of responsibility toward continuing charitable giving. For instance, through such mechanisms as endowments, or waqf, that provide for charitable giving or education, Muslims can, after death, also leave behind a legacy of good deeds to benefit others.

Creating a Halal Estate Plan and Will (Wasiyyah)

An essential aspect of long-term financial planning in Islam is the preparation of a halal estate plan, which includes creating a valid will, known as wasiyyah. The Quran provides clear guidance on the distribution of wealth after death, and Muslims must comply with these rules to ensure their wealth is allocated fairly among their heirs.

In Islam, the distribution of an estate is governed by Faraid, the Islamic law of inheritance. This law outlines the specific shares that must be given to family members, such as parents, children, and spouses, ensuring that wealth is distributed justly and equitably.

As stated in the Quran: "Allah commands you regarding your children's [inheritance]: for a male, what is equal to the share of two females. But if there are [only] daughters, two or more, their share is two-thirds of the estate. If there is only one, her share is half. For parents, a sixth share of the inheritance to each if the deceased left children" (Quran 4:11)

These guidelines are designed to prevent disputes and ensure that wealth is distributed in accordance with Allah's wisdom.

However, besides the mandatory shares prescribed by Faraid, Muslims are allowed to bequeath up to one-third of their estate to non-heirs, such as charitable causes or distant relatives. This bequest must be clearly stated in the wasiyyah and should not exceed the one-third limit.

The Prophet Muhammad (PBUH) emphasised this when he said, "One third, and one third is much" (Bukhari)

This portion can be used to support charitable organisations, educational initiatives, or any other cause that aligns with Islamic principles, ensuring that part of one's wealth continues to generate good deeds even after death.

Creating a halal estate plan involves more than just writing a will. It also includes appointing trustworthy executors who can ensure that the estate is distributed according to Islamic law, settling any debts the deceased owes, and providing for any outstanding obligations, such as unpaid Zakat or missed prayers. It is also important to ensure that all legal documents comply with Islamic and local legal requirements to avoid potential disputes or legal challenges after death.

In many cases, Muslims may wish to set up charitable endowments (waqf) as part of their estate planning. A waqf allows individuals to allocate a portion of their wealth for ongoing charitable purposes, such as building schools, mosques, or hospitals. This can be a powerful way to leave behind a legacy that benefits the community long after the individual has passed away.

Finally, it is essential to regularly review and update the estate plan to ensure it reflects any changes in family circumstances, financial situation, or legal requirements. This proactive approach helps prevent complications and ensures that the wealth is distributed in a manner that aligns with Islamic values and principles.

Setting long-term financial goals and creating a halal estate plan is crucial to Islamic financial responsibility. By preserving wealth, planning for intergenerational transfer, and ensuring that assets are distributed in accordance with Islamic guidelines, Muslims can leave behind a legacy that benefits their descendants and the broader community. The preparation of a wasiyyah and the integration of charitable giving into one's estate plan allow Muslims to not only fulfil their obligations to their family but also earn ongoing rewards through continued acts of charity and support for good causes. Through thoughtful and responsible financial planning, Muslims can ensure that their wealth serves both their immediate family and the wider ummah, leaving behind a lasting legacy of goodness and justice.

Embracing Islamic Principles for Financial Success

Islam provides a comprehensive framework for managing wealth that integrates spiritual, ethical, and financial principles. Embracing these teachings leads to financial success that is grounded in justice, charity, and personal growth. By adhering to Islamic financial ethics, Muslims can achieve prosperity in both this life and the Hereafter, ensuring their wealth is beneficial for themselves, their families, and their communities.

Summary of Key Lessons on Money Mindset and Wealth Management in Islam

The Islamic approach to wealth is deeply rooted in balance, fairness, and social responsibility. Throughout this exploration of financial planning, wealth preservation, and charitable giving, several key lessons emerge:

Wealth as a Trust from Allah (SWT): Islam teaches that wealth is not owned by individuals but is a trust from Allah. Muslims are its custodians and must use it responsibly. This means avoiding greed, selfishness, and extravagance while ensuring that the basic needs of oneself and one's family are met.

Charity as a Means of Purification: Both Zakat (obligatory alms) and Sadaqah (voluntary charity) are essential in purifying wealth and promoting social equity. Zakat ensures the redistribution of wealth, supporting the less fortunate and upholding social justice, while regular Sadaqah brings spiritual benefits and increases blessings in one's wealth.

Prohibition of Riba (Interest): Islamic financial management strictly forbids transactions involving riba (interest), which is seen as exploitative and unjust. Instead, Muslims are encouraged to engage in halal business activities, investments, and trade that promote fairness and ethical practices.

Wealth Preservation and Long-Term Planning: Islam emphasises the importance of preserving wealth for future generations. Setting clear financial goals, making halal investments, and planning for intergenerational wealth transfer are essential steps in ensuring that wealth continues to benefit families and society in the long term.

Estate Planning and Islamic Will (Wasiyyah): Creating a halal estate plan and will is crucial in ensuring that wealth is distributed according to Islamic guidelines after death. This ensures justice among heirs and provides opportunities for ongoing charitable contributions.

Accountability and Avoidance of Wastefulness: Muslims are held accountable for how they earn, spend, and distribute wealth. Islam encourages moderation and cautions against wastefulness, encouraging Muslims to make wise financial decisions that benefit both themselves and others.

Committing to Lifelong Learning and Practice of Islamic Financial Ethics

Achieving financial success in Islam is not a one-time effort but a lifelong commitment. Muslims are encouraged to continually seek knowledge about Islamic finance and apply its principles daily.

> As the Prophet Muhammad (PBUH) said, "Seeking knowledge is an obligation upon every Muslim" (Ibn Majah)

With lifelong learning, Muslims learn of new developments in the financial world and adjust their practices to new situations while remaining faithful to the Islamic call. They might do so by reading the Quran and Hadith, attending seminars on finance based on Islam or seeking qualified scholars to guide them; all these will increase their understanding of wealth management and apply it to their best advantage while remaining faithful to their religion.

By constantly practising the principles of Islamic financial ethics, such as honesty, transparency, justice, and charity, Muslims lay down a foundation for true financial success that benefits them in this life and guarantees rewards for all eternity in the Hereafter. This commitment to ethical financial conduct ensures that every transaction, investment, or act of giving is in harmony with the teachings of Islam, imbuing their financial endeavours with blessings and peace.

In conclusion, embracing Islamic principles for financial prosperity speaks of more than the acquisition of wealth; it speaks of a balanced, responsible, and generous life. After all, by conscious financial planning, frequent charity, and sincere compliance with Islam's guidelines, Muslims could really acquire prosperity and leave behind a rich legacy true to their faith and values.

Chapter Twelve

Conclusion

Achieving financial freedom while adhering to Islamic principles is not only possible but deeply rewarding. By aligning your financial practices with the ethical guidelines set by Islam, you can break free from money blocks, build wealth responsibly, and contribute to the well-being of your family, community, and future generations.

Throughout this book, we've explored the critical connection between faith and finances. Each chapter provided actionable steps rooted in Islamic teachings, from overcoming limiting beliefs and adopting an abundance mindset to managing debt and investing in a halal manner. By implementing these strategies, you can create a balanced and prosperous life that honours both your worldly responsibilities and spiritual values.

Islam teaches us that wealth is a blessing and a trust from Allah (SWT), and with it comes the responsibility of stewardship (Amanah). Whether through budgeting, earning a halal income, or giving generously through Zakat and Sadaqah, you are empowered to handle your resources in a way that benefits both yourself and others.

Financial freedom is not just about having more money. It's about peace of mind, knowing that your financial choices are in harmony with your faith. It's about letting go of fear and scarcity, trusting Allah's (SWT) provision, and embracing a proactive approach to wealth-building.

As you continue your journey, remember that true wealth lies in contentment, gratitude, and the willingness to share your blessings with others. By integrating the principles of Islam into your financial life, you pave the way for material success, spiritual growth, and fulfilment. May this book serve as a guide to help you unlock your financial potential, overcome obstacles, and achieve lasting prosperity in this life and the hereafter.

Embrace wealth with faith, and let your financial freedom flourish.

Find Out More

Website: www.barakahinbusiness.com

Socials: @barakahinbusiness

If you enjoyed this book, kindly leave a review to help expand our reach so others may benefit also.